THE FAMOUS CHICKEN BASEBALL QUIZ BOOK

The Famous Chicken Baseball Quiz Book

by

Ted Giannoulas
The Famous Chicken
and
Andy Strasberg

Slawson/The Word Shop, Inc.
San Diego

Copyright ©1984 by Ted Giannoulas and Andy Strasberg

All rights reserved. No part of this publication may be reproduced or transmitted in any form or by any means, electronic or mechanical, including photocopy, recording, or any information storage and retrieval system, without permission in writing from the publisher.

First edition

Library of Congress Card Catalog Number 84-050261
ISBN 0-915391-00-7

Cover and Book Design by Doug Armstrong

Printed in the United States of America

Table of Contents

Section I:	**Questions**	1
	Flying Feathers	3
	On the Wing	13
	Fowl Ball	23
	Scratch Hits	33
	Bawks	41
	Goose Eggs	51
Section II:	**Famous Name Photo Game**	61
Section III:	**Answers**	71
Section IV:	**Answer Worksheet**	121

Section I
Questions

Flying Feathers

1 A player once won the Most Valuable Player Award the year after being traded.

TRUE or FALSE

2 Who was the player to win the Most Valuable Player award twice with the greatest number of years (11 years) separating the achievement?

A. Ted Williams
B. Babe Ruth
C. Willie Mays
D. Pete Rose

3 Name the only player to be thrown out of a major league game and yet never play in one.
   A. Walt Alston
   B. Arnie Cardillo
   C. Bill Sharman
   D. Tom Lasorda

4 Who was the only Heisman Trophy winner to play major league baseball?
   A. Jackie Robinson
   B. Bill Skowron
   C. Vic Janowicz
   D. Greasy Neal

5 Name the pitcher who started two All-Star games in the same year.
   A. Don Drysdale
   B. Whitey Ford
   C. Juan Marichal
   D. Bob Gibson

6 What is the record for triple plays by one club in one season?
   A. 3
   B. 6
   C. 9
   D. 10

7 What is the record for the most consecutive games postponed due to weather in a season?
   A. 3
   B. 5
   C. 7
   D. 9

8 Which of the following players hit the most home runs at age 40?

- A. Ted Williams
- B. Hank Aaron
- C. Carl Yastrzemski
- D. Stan Musial

9 How many times did Mickey Mantle hit a home run both left- and right-handed in the same game?

- A. 3
- B. 5
- C. 10
- D. 17

10 When was the first time a club used numbers on their uniforms?

- A. 1883
- B. 1901
- C. 1929
- D. 1931

11 Who caught Roger Maris' 61st home run?

- A. Tom House
- B. Pedro Ramos
- C. Sal Durante
- D. Johnny Blanchard

12 Name the only player to ever pinch it for Hank Aaron while he played for the Braves.

- A. Carrol Hardy
- B. Mike Lum
- C. Roland Office
- D. Bob Horner

6 THE BASEBALL QUIZ BOOK

13 The New York Mets once had a pitcher who took 12 years to win his second game as a Met after he won his first. Can you name him?

A. Bob L. Miller
B. Al Jackson
C. Tom Seaver
D. Bob G. Miller

14 Who was the first catcher for the Dodgers to lead the team in both RBI's and homers in the same season?

A. Roy Campanella
B. John Roseborro
C. Joe Ferguson
D. Steve Yeager

15 In Joe Pignatano's last career at bat in 1962 as a Mets player he:

A. Hit a grand slam
B. Hit into a triple play
C. Was beaned
D. Hit the last ground rule double in the Polo Grounds

16 Mel Ott holds the record for most intentional base on balls for an extra inning game. How many?

A. Three
B. Four
C. Five
D. Six

17 Which team holds the record for the most consecutive games in which they hit at least one home run?

   A. 1957 Braves
   B. 1941 Yankees
   C. 1965 Twins
   D. 1978 Red Sox

18 Who said, "It's an old touche, but the cream always rises to the top."

   A. Casey Stengle
   B. Doug Rader
   C. Danny Ozark
   D. Jerry Coleman

19 Prior to 1950, only one player (Ginger Beaumont - 1902) won the batting title (.357) but did not have at least one home run.

   TRUE or FALSE

20 Which group of players hit home runs in the World Series for both American and National League teams?

   A. Gene Tenace, Elston Howard, Reggie Smith, Frank Robinson
   B. Enos Slaughter, Frank Robinson, Roger Maris, Bill Skowron
   C. Bernie Carbo, Roger Maris, Gene Tenace, Frank Robinson
   D. Bill Skowron, Elston Howard, Reggie Smith, Frank Robinson

8 THE BASEBALL QUIZ BOOK

21 What is the record for the most errors committed during a ball game?
- A. 20
- B. 25
- C. 30
- D. 40

22 Match the player with their real first name.
- A. Albert
- B. Fred
- C. Lynn
- D. George
- E. Thomas
- F. Don

1. Nolan Ryan
2. Tom Seaver
3. Richie Ashburn
4. Sparky Lyle
5. Mike Shannon
6. Dixie Walker

23 In 1955, a player with the Brooklyn Dodgers managed to hit home runs for each of his only three hits. Can you name him?
- A. Don Zimmer
- B. Clem Labine
- C. Don Drysdale
- D. Sandy Koufax

24 Who holds the record for slugging percentage and total bases in one season (100 or more games)?
- A. Babe Ruth
- B. Lou Gerhig
- C. Jim Rice
- D. Mike Schmidt

25 Pete Gray was the only one-armed baseball player in the majors. How many times do you think he struck out when he played for St. Louis Browns in 1945? (Hint: He went to bat over 200 times.)

A. 11
B. 54
C. 110
D. 127

26 What is the record for hitting into the most triple plays in a player's career?

A. Three by Jackie Jensen
B. Four by Brooks Robinson
C. Five by Ernie Lombardi
D. Six by Hank Aaron

27 A pitcher cannot be listed as both right and left-handed in the Baseball Encyclopedia.

TRUE or FALSE

28 What is the record for most players used by one club in the National League over an entire season?

A. 43 — San Diego Padres 1969
B. 47 — Montreal Expos 1972
C. 50 — Houston Astros 1965
D. 54 — New York Mets 1967

29 In 1962, Mets Manager Casey Stengel was quoted as saying, "We was going to give you a birthday cake, but we figured you'd drop it." Who was he referring to?

A. Rod Kanehl
B. Dick Stuart
C. Marv Throneberry
D. Felix Mantilla

30 What is the record number of pitchers used in one 9-inning game by two teams?
   A. 7
   B. 12
   C. 14
   D. 16

31 This Hall of Famer, while pitching in 1914, had an ERA of 9.00. Who is he?
   A. Babe Ruth
   B. Ernie Shore
   C. Tris Speaker
   D. Walter Johnson

32 Has there ever been a pitcher who has both won and lost 20 games in the same season?

   YES or NO

33 How many plate appearances must a batter have to qualify for a batting title?
   A. 360
   B. 365
   C. 502
   D. 483

34 Who was the winning pitcher in the famous game when Bobby Thompson hit his 1951 playoff home run to win the pennant for the New York Giants?
   A. Ralph Branca
   B. Don Newcome
   C. Sal Maglie
   D. Larry Jansen

35 What would happen if all 25 players were used in one game with the last nine on the field and there was an injury?
- A. Reschedule
- B. Resume play the next available date
- C. Revert to the previous inning if after 5th inning, otherwise suspend the game.
- D. The short-handed team would forfeit.

36 Rocky Colavito:
- A. Hit over 375 homers
- B. Pitched for the Yankees
- C. Stole at least 20 bases in his career
- D. Never led the American League in homers.

37 There are two pitchers who have won 100 games in both leagues. One of them is Cy Young. Name the other.
- A. Vida Blue
- B. Don Sutton
- C. Tommy John
- D. Jim Bunning

38 Has anyone participated in more consecutive major league games than Lou Gehrig's string of 2,130 ball games?

YES or NO

39 Has anyone ever caught a touchdown pass from Y.A. Tittle and hit a home run off Sandy Koufax?

YES or NO

40 Has a pitcher ever won 20 games or more in one season without losing one?

YES or NO

41 Is it possible for a game to be won by a team without a pitcher getting credit for a win or loss?

YES or NO

42 Who was the youngest player ever to appear in an American League game?
- A. Donald McDonald
- B. Car Scheib
- C. Willey Joel
- D. Don Regean

43 The most errors committed in one season by one player is:
- A. 48
- B. 54
- C. 92
- D. 106

44 Which is the leading trio for homers on one team in one season?
- A. Schmidt, Luzinski, Diaz
- B. Ruth, Gehrig, Lazzeri
- C. Mantle, Maris, Skowron
- D. Horner, Murphy, Chamblis

45 Which major league player was born the day Bobby Thomson hit his historic playoff home run October 3, 1951?
- A. Pete Vuckovich
- B. Bump Wills
- C. Dave Winfield
- D. None of the above

On the Wing

46 What was the length of the shortest major league game?

- A. 51 minutes
- B. 1 hour 5 minutes
- C. 1 hour 21 minutes
- D. 1 hour 48 minutes

47 What is the record for most balks by a pitcher in a season?

- A. 6
- B. 8
- C. 10
- D. 12

48 Who was the youngest manager of a major league club?

A. Tony LaRussa
B. Lou Boudreau
C. Roger Peckinpaugh
D. Frank Quilici

49 Of all the bonafide hitters (no tricks, honest) in Cooperstown, which Hall of Famer had the lowest career batting average?

A. Tommy McCarthy
B. Johnny Evers
C. Ray Schalk
D. Bobby Wallace

50 What team left the most players on base in one season?

A. '69 Pilots
B. '69 Giants
C. '41 Browns
D. '76 Padres

51 Who was the oldest National Leaguer to win the batting crown?

A. Rogers Hornsby
B. Stan Musial
C. Honus Wagner
D. Pete Rose

52 What is the record for most consecutive homers in one inning by a National League team?

A. 3
B. 4
C. 5
D. 6

53 A pitcher can win 20 games and have an ERA of more than 5.

TRUE or FALSE

54 What team had the highest batting average for one season?
- A. 1927 Yankees
- B. 1979 Pirates
- C. 1959 Dodgers
- D. 1894 Phillies

55 Who replaced Lou Gehrig at first base after Gehrig completed his 2,130th game?
- A. Joe Collins
- B. Joe Pepitone
- C. Bill "Moose" Skowron
- D. Babe Dahlgren

56 The score is 1-1 in the bottom of the ninth with the bases loaded. The batter hits a ground rule double. Is the final score:
- A. 2 to 1
- B. 3 to 1
- C. 4 to 1
- D. 5 to 1

57 What was the name of the center fielder for the Indians who played in the game when Bob Feller threw his no-hitter against the Yankees on April 30, 1946? Hint: He is now a member of the Hall of Fame.
- A. Pat Seery
- B. Rocky Colavito
- C. Felix Mackiewicz
- D. Bob Lemon

58 The Mets played a game against the Giants in 1964 that went 23 innings; a game against the Astros in 1968 that went 24 innings; and a game against the 1974 Cardinals that went 25 innings. Would you believe that in all three games the home plate umpire was the same man? Who was it?

A. Ed Sudol
B. Doug Harvey
C. Satch Davidson
D. Eric Gregg

59 Who was the very first playing manager?

A. Casey Stengel
B. Lou Boudreau
C. John McGraw
D. Connie Mack

60 Hall of Famer Dave Bancroft's nickname was:

A. Piano Legs
B. Grey Eagle
C. Ban
D. Beauty

61 What team holds the record (starting from 1900) for most runs scored in a single inning?

A. 1952 Dodgers
B. 1927 Yanks
C. 1955 Dodgers
D. 1982 Braves

62 In 1950, the league leader in the American League in stolen bases had 15 thefts.

TRUE or FALSE

63 Which of the following teams' former players who are in the Hall of Fame cannot field a complete 9-man team at each position?

A. Giants
B. Yankees
C. Cubs

64 What is the record for triples in one game by a player?

A. Three
B. Four
C. Five
D. Six

65 Who was the first player to hit homers both right- and left-handed in the same game?

A. Mickey Mantle
B. Pete Rose
C. Augie Galan
D. Max Carey

66 Who owns the record for the most major league hits by a player in one season?

A. Pete Rose
B. Ty Cobb
C. George Sisler
D. Rod Carew

67 What team was been shut out the most times in one season?

A. 1908 St. Louis Cardinals
B. 1980 Toronto Blue Jays
C. 1945 St. Louis Browns
D. 1970 Milwaukee Brewers

68 Who was the first player to hit a home run during a night game?

A. Jim Bottomley
B. Sam Byrd
C. Ernie Lombardi
D. Babe Herman

69 What is the most number of hits a player collected in one game (extra innings count)

A. 7
B. 8
C. 9
D. 10

70 Which team made the most double plays in one season and in what year did this occur?

A. 1959 Dodgers
B. 1949 Athletics
C. 1969 Mets
D. 1966 Pirates

71 How long was the longest game?

A. 5 hours 23 minutes
B. 6 hours 23 minutes
C. 7 hours 23 minutes
D. 8 hours 23 minutes

72 Who said, "When I'm through managing, I'm going to open up a kindergarten."

A. Earl Weaver
B. Sparky Anderson
C. Ralph Houk
D. Billy Martin

73 If the infield fly rule is called and the ball is dropped in foul territory, is the batter still out?

YES or NO

74 Who has the record for throwing a ball the greatest distance?
- A. Rocky Colavito
- B. Glen E. Gorbous
- C. Peter Briante
- D. Howard Frank

75 Who holds the record for hitting into the most double plays in a season?
- A. Brooks Robinson
- B. Jackie Jensen
- C. Hank Aaron
- D. Pete Rose

76 Who hit the first home run off of Tom Seaver?
- A. Lee May
- B. Jerry May
- C. Carlos May
- D. Dave May

77 Match the players with their real first names.

A.	Harry	1.	Gene Conley
B.	Arnold	2.	Sherm Lollar
C.	John	3.	Cookie Lavagetto
D.	Arthur	4.	Mickey Owen
E.	Donald	5.	Randy Hundley
F.	Cecil	6.	Lee May

20 THE BASEBALL QUIZ BOOK

78 Identify the only major league player to be active in Babe Ruth's last year as a player (1935) and Hank Aaron's first year (1954).
   A. Satchel Paige
   B. Billy Herman
   C. Phil Cavarretta
   D. Al Lopez

79 Was there ever a pitcher who was named Rookie of the Year, won the Most Valuable Player and also won the Cy Young Award?

   YES or NO

80 What was Eddie Gaedel's uniform number?
   A. 1/4
   B. 1/8
   C. 0
   D. 1

81 Name the player who hit into the first all Cuban triple play.
   A. Billy Martin
   B. Dick Williams
   C. Sparky Anderson
   D. Whitey Herzog

82 Name the only pitcher to face both Babe Ruth and Mickey Mantle in a regular season game.
   A. Satchel Paige
   B. Al Benton
   C. Early Wynn
   D. Red Barrett

83 Who was the first Designated Hitter ever to hit a home run?
- A. Tony Oliva
- B. Ron Blomberg
- C. Gates Brown
- D. Jim Hart

84 What is the record for most base hits by a player in one inning?
- A. 2
- B. 3
- C. 4
- D. 5

85 Pitcher Clyde Shoun's career spanned from 1935 to '49 in which he won 73 games. What was his nickname?
- A. Moon
- B. Goon
- C. Ram
- D. Hardrock

86 What is the record for most strike-outs for both clubs in one game since 1900?
- A. 15
- B. 28
- C. 31
- D. 35

87 What is the record for most times reached base consecutively by a batter?
- A. 7
- B. 9
- C. 12
- D. 14

88 Has a player ever appeared in the World Series for more than two different teams in his career?

YES or NO

89 Name the first player to object legally to a trade and then get his wish to be traded to another team.

A. Duke Snider
B. Andy Messersmith
C. Curt Flood
D. Ron Santo

90 Name the player who went in to replace Tony Kubek in the 1960 seventh game of the World Series after the Yankee shortstop was hit in the throat with a bad hop grounder.

A. Billy Gardner
B. Andy Carey
C. Joe DeMaestri
D. Clete Boyer

91 Has there ever been a player to hit 10 or fewer home runs but manage 100 or more RBIs in one season?

YES or NO

92 Who was the Houston Astros' first 20 game winner?

A. Denny Lemaster
B. Don Wilson
C. Fred Gladding
D. Larry Dierker

Fowl Ball

93 Name the San Francisco Giant who hit a grand slam in his first major league game.
- A. Jack Clark
- B. Bobby Bonds
- C. Chili Davis
- D. Dave Kingman

94 What is the record number of teams that one player played for in a season?
- A. 4
- B. 5
- C. 6
- D. 7

24 THE BASEBALL QUIZ BOOK

95 Which of the following players did not collect 20 doubles, triples and home runs in the same season during his career?

- A. Willie Mays
- B. George Brett
- C. Jim Rice
- D. Jim Bottomley

96 What is the N.L. record for most hits by a player in his first game?

- A. 4
- B. 5
- C. 6
- D. 7

97 Name the only pitcher who was involved in decision of both the Branca-Thomson playoff homer game and Don Larsen's perfect World Series game.

- A. Don Newcombe
- B. Sal Maglie
- C. Larry Jensen
- D. Johnny Podres

98 What did Johnny Vander Meer do in the next ball game following his two no-hitters?

- A. Lasted two innings and then gave up 6 hits.
- B. The first hitter he faced in the next game singled.
- C. After walking the first two hitters, he was taken out.
- D. Fired more than three innings of hitless ball.

FOWL BALL 25

99 What is the name of the pitcher with the most consecutive victories?

A. Steve Carlton
B. Fernando Valenzuela
C. Carl Hubbell
D. Cy Young

100 Who had the fewest strike-outs in his most productive home run season?

A. Maris
B. Ruth
C. Aaron
D. Mays

101 Name the first pitcher to wear glasses.

A. "Eye Chart" Davidson
B. William H. White
C. Four Eyes Morrison
D. Spec Shea

102 Which of the following players during their careers got more walks in a season than hits:

A. Eddie Stanky
B. Ted Williams
C. Jimmy Wynn
D. Lou Brock

103 Which of the following players never hit for the cycle?

A. Babe Herman
B. Babe Ruth
C. Bob Meusel
D. Lou Brock

104
Match the following 1931 National League batting averages with the correct players.

A. .3489 1. Jim Bottomley
B. .3486 2. Bill Terry
C. .3482 3. Chick Hafey
D. .337   4. Chuck Klein

105
Name the pitcher who replaced Herb Score after he was hit in the eye by a line drive off the bat of Gil McDougal in that unforgettable 1957 game.

A. Don Mossi
B. Bud Daley
C. Early Wynn
D. Bob Lemon

106
How many left-handed throwing catchers have there been in major league baseball?

A. 5
B. 9
C. 14
D. 21

107
Can you name three Dodger coaches from 1965 who went on to be major league managers?

108
Which pitcher walked the most players in a regular season game?

A. Ryne Duren
B. Nolan Ryan
C. Bruno Hess
D. Dick Freeman

FOWL BALL 27

109 The Chicago White Sox hold the record for fewest homers in one season. How many?

A. 0
B. 1
C. 2
D. 3

110 What is the name of the team whose players struck out the most times in one season?

A. '82 Mets
B. '68 Giants
C. '79 Blue Jays
D. '72 Cubs

111 Joe DiMaggio owns the longest hitting streak in baseball and, of course, for the Yankees, with 56 games. Which of the following Yankees has the second longest streak (29 games) for the American League Team?

A. Dave Winfield
B. Joe Gordon
C. Thurman Munson
D. Babe Ruth

112 What is the record for a team's lowest composite batting average for one season?

A. .180
B. .207
C. .216
D. .231

113 Has a player ever assisted in more than one triple play in a season?

YES or NO

28 THE BASEBALL QUIZ BOOK

114 What is the record for getting the most hits with the same number of at-bats?
- A. 6 for 6
- B. 7 for 7
- C. 8 for 8
- D. 10 for 10

115 How many pitchers have thrown two no-hitters in the same season?
- A. 5
- B. 10
- C. 12
- D. 15

116 What pitcher hit the most home runs in his career?
- A. Don Drysdale
- B. Bob Gibson
- C. Wes Ferrell
- D. Don Newcombe

117 Only one of the following pitchers lost a World Series game. Which one?
- A. Jerry Koosman
- B. Lefty Gomez
- C. Catfish Hunter
- D. Herb Pennock

118 What do the following names have in common with baseball: Chicken Wolf, Bob Unglaub, Patsy Tebeau, Muddy Ruel, Vedie Himsl, Judge Fuchs, Ossie Bluege, and Hugo Bezdek?
- A. All were major league managers
- B. Each hit 5 doubles in one game
- C. Each had one major league at bat and struck out
- D. All roomed with Babe Ruth

119 What is the record for most runs scored by a team in one game?

- A. 23
- B. 29
- C. 37
- D. 53

120 What team holds the record for the fewest errors committed in one season?

- A. '59 Dodgers
- B. '64 Orioles
- C. '78 Red Sox
- D. '78 Yankees

121 What player finished second for the home run title the most times?

- A. Mel Ott
- B. Ted Williams
- C. Hank Aaron
- D. Reggie Jackson

122 Who holds the seasonal and single game record for most assists by an outfielder?

- A. Chuck Klein
- B. Jimmy Piersall
- C. Jim Rice
- D. Dave Winfield

123 Has a player ever stolen first base?

- A. YES or NO

124 Which World Series saw each game end in a shutout?

- A. 1905
- B. 1931
- C. 1944
- D. 1961

125
Who was the first black coach in the National League?

- A. Frank Robinson
- B. Ernie Banks
- C. Jim Gilliam
- D. Deacon Jones

126
Name the 1948 player who missed winning the Triple Crown by one home run.

- A. Ted Williams
- B. Stan Musial
- C. Yogi Berra
- D. Joe DiMaggio

127
What is the record for a catcher's assists in one season?

- A. 114
- B. 168
- C. 214
- D. 268

128
Has a club ever won a World Series without having a player hit .300 during the season?

YES or NO

129
Back in the 1960's, two teams traded managers. What teams were involved?

- A. A's & Orioles
- B. Tigers & Indians
- C. Red Sox & Tigers
- D. Braves & Phillies

130
Has a club ever played an entire season without a manager?

YES or NO

FOWL BALL 31

131 Who was the first player to hit a home run in the Houston Astrodome?
- A. Mickey Mantle
- B. Doug Rader
- C. Sonny Jackson
- D. Willie Mays

132 What is the greatest number of games lost by a pitcher in one season?
- A. 24
- B. 27
- C. 36
- D. 48

133 What is the longest game ever played (n innings)?
- A. 24
- B. 26
- C. 28
- D. 29

134 What is the record for most consecutive innings a team has gone without giving up a run?
- A. 24
- B. 36
- C. 48
- D. 56

135 How many home runs did the entire Washington team hit while playing at home in 1945?
- A. None
- B. 1
- C. 2
- D. 3

32 THE BASEBALL QUIZ BOOK

136 Which pitcher pitched the most innings in one season?

A. William White
B. Cy Young
C. Walter Johnson
D. Grover Cleveland Alexander

137 Which player hit the most home runs in a major league park away from home (one season)?

A. Lou Gehrig
B. Mickey Mantle
C. Harry Heilman
D. Hank Aaron

138 Which of the following players holds the single season home run record for left fielders?

A. Babe Ruth
B. Ralph Kiner
C. Ted Williams
D. Willie Stargell

139 Is there a record for consecutive postponed games in a season?

YES or NO

140 What is the record for fewest chances by a first baseman in a game?

A. 0
B. 1
C. 2
D. 3

Scratch Hits

141 Which pitcher has the best "strikeout rate" per game for one season?
- A. Steve Carlton
- B. Walter Johnson
- C. Sam McDowell
- D. Nolan Ryan

142 Hank Aaron broke Babe Ruth's career home run mark of 714. But how many home runs in a lifetime was the record that Ruth broke?
- A. 92
- B. 126
- C. 312
- D. 421

34 THE BASEBALL QUIZ BOOK

143 Is there a time limit between pitches?
YES or NO

144 What is the record for most players left on base by two teams in a regulation nine-inning game?
- A. 0
- B. 10
- C. 20
- D. 30

145 Has a player ever hit 40 home runs or more in less than 400 at-bats in one season?
YES or NO

146 What are the lowest recorded statistics in both the National and American Leagues combined to win one of the three major hitting categories (average, home runs, RBI)?
- A. .283, 2 homers, 58 RBIs
- B. .290, 4 homers, 60 RBIs
- C. .301, 6 homers, 71 RBIs
- D. .310, 15 homers, 92 RBIs

147 Who was the first player to pinch hit safely 20 times in a season?
- A. Smokey Burgess
- B. Kurt Bevacqua
- C. Johnny Mize
- D. Ed Coleman

148 This Hall of Famer pitched a total of three games and totaled five innings while giving up six hits and two walks. He first pitched in 1918 and again in 1925. Name him.
  A. Ty Cobb
  B. Ed Roush
  C. Sam Crawford
  D. Casey Stengel

149 There was once a no-hitter pitched on opening day of a season as well as one on the last day of that season.

TRUE or FALSE

150 Who was the only Yankee to win two batting titles of the players listed below?
  A. Mickey Mantle
  B. Joe DiMaggio
  C. Babe Ruth
  D. Lou Gehrig

151 The situation is the last half of the ninth inning in a game that has no score but the bases are loaded. The count on the batter is 3-2. The next pitch is a sweeping curve and the batter takes a vicious cut. He misses the ball but it cuts in and hits him on the side. Is it:
  A. Do-over
  B. Strike
  C. Hit Batsman
  D. Ball

36 THE BASEBALL QUIZ BOOK

152 How many times has a National League pitcher struck out four batters in one inning?

- A. 2
- B. 4
- C. 6
- D. 8

153 Which player stole home the most times in a single season?

- A. Pete Reiser
- B. Ty Cobb
- C. Lou Brock
- D. Rod Carew

154 What is the record for most pitchers used in a game by one and two teams?

- A. 9 and 14
- B. 6 and 11
- C. 14 and 16
- D. 11 and 13

155 What is the record for hitting an inside the park home run in one game by a player?

- A. 1
- B. 2
- C. 3
- D. 4

156 Who was the first player to pinch hit for Babe Ruth?

- A. Tris Speaker
- B. Harry Hooper
- C. Duffy Lewis
- D. Ernie Shore

157 What is the record for pitching the most relief innings in one game?

   A. 12
   B. 14-2/3
   C. 18-1/3
   D. 20

158 Has there ever been a player who was intentionally walked with the bases loaded?

   YES or NO

159 Who was the first major league player to enter military service in World War I?

   A. Zach Wheat
   B. Casey Stengel
   C. Harry M. Gowdy
   D. Paul Zimmerman

160 What is the major league record for sacrifice hits in one season by a player?

   A. 30
   B. 31
   C. 52
   D. 67

161 Has a player ever won the home run title in either league without striking out more than ten times?

   YES or NO

162 What is the record for the most errors by one team in a single inning in baseball history?

   A. 4
   B. 5
   C. 7
   D. 13

38 THE BASEBALL QUIZ BOOK

163 Who was the first black pitcher to win a World Series game?

A. Joe Black
B. Don Newcombe
C. Dan Blankhead
D. Bob Gibson

164 What is the record for most base hits in a 9-inning game by one team?

A. 23
B. 32
C. 36
D. 43

165 What is the record for most errors in one game by a team?

A. 22
B. 24
C. 31
D. 36

166 Is it possible in a World Series for two pitchers to win three games a piece while another pitcher wins two?

YES or NO

167 What is the name of the last white player to lead the American League in stolen bases in one season prior to 1975?

A. Mickey Mantle
B. Jackie Jensen
C. Albie Pearson
D. Jim Landis

168 Has any player ever hit a home run in his first two at-bats?

YES or NO

169 Since what year were umpires permitted to wear glasses?
- A. 1959
- B. 1965
- C. 1971
- D. 1974

170 How many unassisted triple plays have been executed in the majors?
- A. 3
- B. 6
- C. 8
- D. 10

171 Which team holds the record for most RBIs in a season?
- A. 1927 Yankees
- B. 1932 Yankees
- C. 1936 Yankees
- D. 1961 Yankees

172 Who holds the record in the major leagues for most games played as a first baseman in a career?
- A. Steve Garvey
- B. Lou Gehrig
- C. Mickey Vernon
- D. Jake Beckley

40 THE BASEBALL QUIZ BOOK

173 This player was the only Hall of Famer to play 1,000 games in both the outfield and infield. He had the exact same number of hits on the road as he did at home. Batting .331 overall, he hit .336 at home and .326 on the road; .340 for day games and .320 for night games. Close examination reveals that during this player's career, he hit .323 in May, .325 in April, .327 in July, .327 in August, .344 in June and .344 in September. Name him.

A. Earl Averill
B. Stan Musial
C. Joe DiMaggio
D. Al Kaline

174 What is the record for the longest string of consecutive extra inning ball games by one team?

A. 5
B. 6
C. 8
D. 9

175 Name the player(s) who hold(s) the season and career records for most assists by an outfielder.

A. Willie Mays and Hank Aaron
B. Mickey Mantle and Babe Ruth
C. Lou Brock and Lou Brock
D. Chuck Klein and Tris Speaker

176 Who was the first pitcher to hit a home run in World Series competition?

A. Bob Gibson
B. Mickey Lolich
C. Jim Bagby
D. Don Drysdale

Bawks

177 Ted Williams earned run average for pitching in the major leagues is 4.50.

TRUE or FALSE

178 Has a player ever hit a homer on the first pitch in his first at-bat in the majors?

YES or NO

179 Babe Ruth took 8,399 at bats to hit his total of 714 home runs. How many homers did Hank Aaron have after 8,399 at bats?

- A. 488
- B. 562
- C. 603
- D. 698

42 THE BASEBALL QUIZ BOOK

180 Considered by many as one of the greatest all-around players, this Hall of Famer played every position except catcher. He appeared in one game as a pitcher in 1900 and another in 1902. Who was this remarkable player?l

A. Ty Cobb
B. Mike Kelly
C. Honus Wagner
D. Rogers Hornsby

181 The scene was Sportsman's Park in St. Louis and the batter was Frank Baumholtz in this 1952 game. The pitcher in question would someday enter into baseball's Hall of Fame. The pitcher threw only one pitch, which Baumholtz hit and the third baseman erred. It was the only pitch this Hall of Famer ever threw in his pitching career. Can you identify him?

A. Willie Mays
B. Stan Musial
C. Duke Snider
D. Ralph Kiner

182 How many times in Gaylord Perry's career has he led the league in strikeouts?

A. 0
B. 4
C. 6
D. 7

183 Has a team ever played nine consecutive doubleheaders?

YES or NO

184 Which of the following teams was the first to have the players' names on the back of the uniforms?

A. 1968 Dodgers
B. 1969 Mets
C. 1960 White Sox
D. 1970 Tigers

185 The same player broke up no-hit bids by Phil Niekro, Sonny Siebert and Jim Rooker in 1970 with a hit in the ninth inning of each game. Who was he?

A. Danny Cater
B. Gene Michael
C. Curt Blefary
D. Horace Clark

186 Who would you guess is the Washington Senator player to lead that team in games played, at bat, runs scored, hits, doubles and triples?

A. Eddie Yost
B. Nick Altrock
C. Mickey Vernon
D. Sam Rice

187 What team holds the record for the most men left on base in a 9-inning game?

A. '73 A's
B. '56 Yankees
C. '65 Twins
D. '30 Red Sox

188 What happens when a player hits a home run but doesn't step on one of the bases going around?
- A. He's credited with the last base he touched.
- B. He's out, if appealed.
- C. It's still a homer.
- D. It's a ground rule double.

189 Has a pitcher ever won 200 or more career games yet never had a 20-game winning season?

YES or NO

190 Name the player whose uncle is Gene Mauch and father was also a major league player.
- A. Buddy Bell
- B. Roy Smalley
- C. Steve Trout
- D. Terry Francona

191 Everyone knows that Hack Wilson has the National League home run mark for one season. Whose record did he break?
- A. Rogers Hornsby
- B. Gabby Hartnett
- C. Babe Herman
- D. Chuck Klein

192 How many career stolen bases do you think Babe Ruth had?
- A. Less than 50
- B. More than 50, but less than 100
- C. More than 100, but less than 150
- D. More than 150

193 What is the team record for the most home runs in one game?

A. 6
B. 8
C. 10
D. 12

194 What is the record for most bases stolen by one player in a single game?

A. 4
B. 6
C. 8
D. 10

195 Since the designated hitter has taken the bat out of the American League pitchers' hands, who was the last American League pitcher to connect for a homer in a regular season game?

A. Catfish Hunter
B. Al Downing
C. Roric Harrison
D. Mel Stottlemyre

196 Did Ted Williams ever hit an inside-the-park home run?

YES or NO

197 What are the American and National League records for sacrifice bunts in one season by a player?

A. AL44   NL34
B. AL43   NL46
C. AL64   NL34
D. AL46   NL43

198 What is the record for most foul ball put-outs by a catcher in one game?

   A. 6
   B. 8
   C. 10
   D. 12

199 What pitcher holds the record for most shutout games thrown in one season?

   A. Fernando Valenzuela
   B. Steve Carlton
   C. Grover Cleveland Alexander
   D. Cy Young

200 Which batter of the following was hit by a pitch the most times in his career?

   A. Frank Robinson
   B. Minnie Minoso
   C. Ron Hunt
   D. Eddie Stanky

201 What is the record for the most pinch hitters in a single nine-inning game by one team?

   A. 7
   B. 9
   C. 12
   D. 13

202 Who was in the on-deck circle when Gil McDougald hit Herb Score in the eye with a line drive in 1957?

   A. Jerry Coleman
   B. Billy Martin
   C. Yogi Berra
   D. Mickey Mantle

203 What Hall of Famer made his final appearance as a pinch hitter in the same game that Babe Ruth hit his 60th home run?

- A. Walter Johnson
- B. Sam Rice
- C. Tris Speaker
- D. Earl Combes

204 Who led the 1969 World Champion Mets in stolen bases during the regular season?

- A. Ed Charles
- B. Tommie Agee
- C. Cleon Jones
- D. Don Clendenon

205 Name these "Old" Hall of Famers:

- A. Charles Radbourn
- B. Charles Comiskey
- C. Burleigh Grimes
- D. Clark Griffith
- E. Bill Klein

1. Old Arbitrator
2. Old Fox
3. Old Hoss
4. Old Roman
5. Old Stubblebeard

206 Who was Darold Knowles of the '74 A's referring to when he said, "There isn't enough mustard in the whole world to cover that hot dog."

- A. Tito Fuentes
- B. Reggie Jackson
- C. Willie Montanez
- D. Kurt Bevacqua

207 Which team owns the longest winning streak?

- A. '16 Giants
- B. '32 Pirates
- C. '54 Indians
- D. '75 Reds

208 While Hank Aaron was hitting his record 755 home runs he did it in many stadiums. Aaron played most of his career in the National League. In how many different parks did he hit home runs in the N.L.?

A. 11
B. 15
C. 18
D. 23

209 What pitcher has the highest lifetime batting average?

A. Don Drysdale
B. Wes Ferrell
C. Bob Gibson
D. Lefty Gomez

210 Name the player (since 1900) who hit the most home runs in the regular major league season during the month of October. (League Championship and World Series don't count.)

A. Dick Stuart
B. Charlie Maxwell
C. Frank Howard
D. Gus Zernial

211 What is the record for triple steals in one game by one club?

A. 1
B. 2
C. 3
D. 4

212 This Harlem Globetrotter went on to pitch for a major league team and also appeared in three different World Series. **Name him.**

213 Everyone knows that Joe DiMaggio holds the record for the longest hitting streak with 56 straight games, but whose record did he break?

A. Willie Keeler
B. Ty Cobb
C. George Sisler
D. Joe Jackson

214 Which of the following managers did not win the World Series in his first full year of managing?

A. Rogers Hornsby
B. Eddie Dyer
C. Ralph Houk
D. Dick Williams

215 How many times did Ted Williams strike out in his career?

A. Less than 500 times
B. Less than 650 times, but more than 500
C. Less than 750 times, but more than 650
D. More than 750 times

216 Of all the players to win the triple crown, who had the best record the year he won the crown?

A. Mickey Mantle
B. Rogers Hornsby
C. Jimmy Fox
D. Chuck Klein

217 What is the record for being awarded first base on catcher's interference for a season?

A. 3
B. 6
C. 9
D. 12

218 Who was the American League's first Designated Hitter?

- A. Jim Hart
- B. Ron Blomberg
- C. Tony Oliva
- D. Cesar Tovar

219 Which pitcher has the record for throwing the most grand slam pitches in one season?

- A. Robin Roberts
- B. Jim Bouton
- C. Ray Narleski
- D. Steve Howe

220 Can you name the only major league player to lead his league in homers, triples, doubles, runs scored, batting average, total bases and slugging average in one season?

- A. George McGovern
- B. Richard Nixon
- C. John Kennedy
- D. Tip O'Neill

221 Match the players with their real first names:

A.	Harry	1.	Nippy Jones
B.	Elijah	2.	Mickey Owen
C.	Cecil	3.	Cookie Lavagetto
D.	Arnold	4.	Pumpsie Green
E.	Vernal	5.	Randy Hundley
F.	George	6.	Birdie Tebbetts

Goose Eggs

222 Name the manager who has managed the most teams in the history of baseball prior to Billy Martin.
- A. Casey Stengel
- B. Dick Williams
- C. Joe Torre
- D. Jimmy Dykes

223 Home Run Baker never hit more than 12 homers in one season.

TRUE or FALSE

224 Which of the following brother combinations did not have one hitting a home run off of the other?
- A. Norm and Larry Sherry
- B. Rick and Wes Ferrel
- C. George and Jesse Stoval
- D. Joe and Phil Niekro

225 What is the record for most bases on balls in a 9-inning game by one club without scoring a run?

A. 5
B. 11
C. 17
D. 23

226 Who holds the record for most positions played by one player in one game?

227 This Hall of Famer's nickname is Pud. Who is he?

A. Joe Kelley
B. John Ward
C. James Galvin
D. Roger Connor

228 Babe Ruth started his career as a pitcher for the Boston Red Sox before seeing time with the Yankees. Ty Cobb was playing at the same time Ruth was a pitcher. Cobb faced Ruth in 13 games. What was the Georgia Peach's average against the Sultan of Swat?

A. .173
B. .280
C. .326
D. .444

229 William Gray established a record for walking consecutive batters in one game. How many?

A. 5
B. 6
C. 7
D. 10

230 What player went in to run for Ted Williams and hit a home run in the same inning?
- A. Caroll Hardy
- B. Jimmy Piersall
- C. Gene Stephens
- D. Marty Keough

231 Name the player who holds the record for hitting into the most double plays in an All-Star game.
- A. Stan Musial
- B. Willie Mays
- C. Joe DiMaggio
- D. Reggie Jackson

232 Who said "I'm probably the only guy who worked for Stengel before and after he was a genius."
- A. Gil Hodges
- B. Warren Spahn
- C. Yogi Berra
- D. Duke Snider

233 Name the only player to be in attendance and in uniform the day Roger Maris hit his 61st and the night Hank Aaron hit his 715th home run.

234 Who said, "I'd rather be the shortest player in the majors than the tallest player in the minors."
- A. Albie Pearson
- B. Eddie Gaedel
- C. Freddie Patek
- D. Phil Rizzuto

235 Only one of the following statements is true. Which one?

A. A female during World War II played for a major league team.
B. Only five World Series games have been rained out once they started.
C. Connie Mack as a manager won more games than he lost.
D. A player was traded for a radio announcer.

236 Which of the following players played on the most teams in the majors?

A. Dick Stuart
B. Dave Kingman
C. Tommy Davis
D. Bert Campaneris

237 Who hit the last home run in Jersey City's Roosevelt Stadium when it served as the Dodgers' "home" park for some games in 1956 and 1957?

A. Gil Hodges
B. Harry Anderson
C. Sparky Anderson
D. Joe Adcock

238 Which of the following players hit the most home runs as a rookie?

A. Frank Robinson
B. Brooks Robinson
C. Jackie Robinson
D. Floyd Robinson

239 Babe Ruth hit two or more homers in one game how many times?

A. 60
B. 61
C. 72
D. 83

240 Which of the following pitchers holds the record for striking out the most batters in one inning (4)?

A. Nolan Ryan
B. Steve Carlton
C. Rich Gossage
D. Don Drysdale

241 Name at least two players whose name spelled backwards would read the same.

242 Consider the following players: Ted Williams, Babe Ruth, Willie Mays, Tony Conigliaro, Mickey Mantle, Roger Maris, and Ralph Kiner. Which of these home run hitters hit his 100th homer at the earliest age?

243 Match the following players with their real first name:

A. George   1. Rick Dempsey
B. James   2. Bucky Dent
C. Dudley   3. Ken Griffey
D. Howard   4. Mike Hargrove
E. Russell   5. Bob Horner
F. John   6. Bruce Sutter

244 What is the all-time major league record for most runs scored by a team in one inning?

A. 15
B. 18
C. 19
D. 20

245 Name the all-time season batting champions in each single position since 1900 with the following averages:

First Base: .420
Second Base: .424
Shortstop: .388
Third Base: .379
Outfield: .420
Catcher: .362
Pitcher: .440

246 Can you imagine a player winning the Triple Crown and being traded the following season? It happened once in the National League. Who was that player?

247 Only once in National League history have the same two players tied for the home run title in two consecutive years.

TRUE or FALSE

248 Cesar Tovar struck out only one player in his career as a pitcher. Which of the following players was it?

A. Mickey Mantle
B. Brooks Robinson
C. Reggie Jackson
D. Harmon Kellebrew

249 Johnny Bench leads all catchers for career put-outs with over 10,000. Which of the following catchers is second on the list?

- A. Bill Dickey
- B. Al Lopez
- C. Bill Freehan
- D. Yogi Berra

250 How many players of the 1951 Yankees became major league managers?

- A. 3
- B. 6
- C. 7
- D. 9

251 A left-handed throwing catcher caught over 1,000 games in the majors.

TRUE or FALSE

252 What is the record for a player striking out the least number of times with a minimum of 150 games played (pitchers not included)?

- A. 0
- B. 2
- C. 3
- D. 4

253 When was the last time a pitcher completed and won both ends of a doubleheader?

- A. 1926
- B. 1932
- C. 1958
- D. 1969

58 THE BASEBALL QUIZ BOOK

254 Babe Ruth hit the first home run at Old Yankee Stadium. Who hit the first round-tripper after it was renovated?

A. Reggie Jackson
B. Thurman Munson
C. Dan Ford
D. George Scott

255 What is the record for most runs given up by one pitcher in a game?

A. 15
B. 20
C. 24
D. 31

256 Name Three "Billys" who are in the Hall of Fame. Remember, not *Bill,* but Billy.

257 Elmer Smith hit the first World Series grand slam in 1920. Who hit the second bases loaded homer in World Series competition? Hint: It took over 25 years to do it.

A. Yogi Berra
B. Mickey Mantle
C. Duke Snider
D. Bobby Richardson

258 Ralph Kiner once made the following statement about which player: "Two thirds of the earth is covered by water, the other one-third is covered by _____."

A. Willie Mays
B. Bobby Bonds
C. Andre Dawson
D. Garry Maddox

259 Who is:

A. Hank Aaron
B. Ted Williams
C. Frank Frisch
D. Bill Klein
E. Dixie Walker
F. Vic Raschi

1. The People's Cherce
2. The Springfield Rifle
3. The Old Arbitrator
4. The Fordham Flash
5. The Kid
6. The Hammer

260 Who said, "Cadillacs are down at the end of the bat."

A. Hank Sauer
B. Ralph Kiner
C. Willie Mays
D. Dale Long

261 What was the name of the first former Little Leaguer to appear in a World Series?

A. Hector Torres
B. Joey Jay
C. Bobby Richardson
D. Bob Cerv

262 Which of the following players was Philadelphia pitcher Curt Simmons referring to when he said "_____ is the only player I have ever seen who goes to sleep at the plate. But trying to sneak a fastball past him is like trying to sneak the sunrise past a rooster."

A. Willie Mays
B. Hank Aaron
C. Ernie Banks
D. Stan Musial

Section II
Famous Name Photo Game

Famous Name
Photo Game

On the following pages are photographs of players and their facial features.

Place the right face under the right cap and identify the ball player.

See number one on page 64 for example.

64 THE BASEBALL QUIZ BOOK

1
Name BABE RUTH
Face E

2
Name _____
Face _____

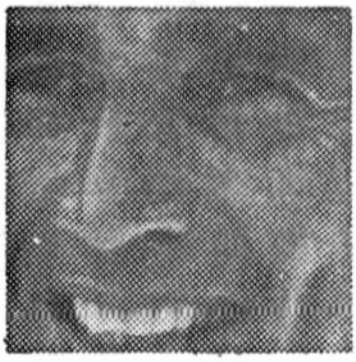

A.

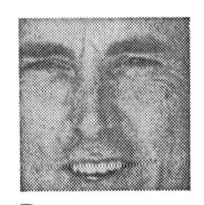

B.

C.

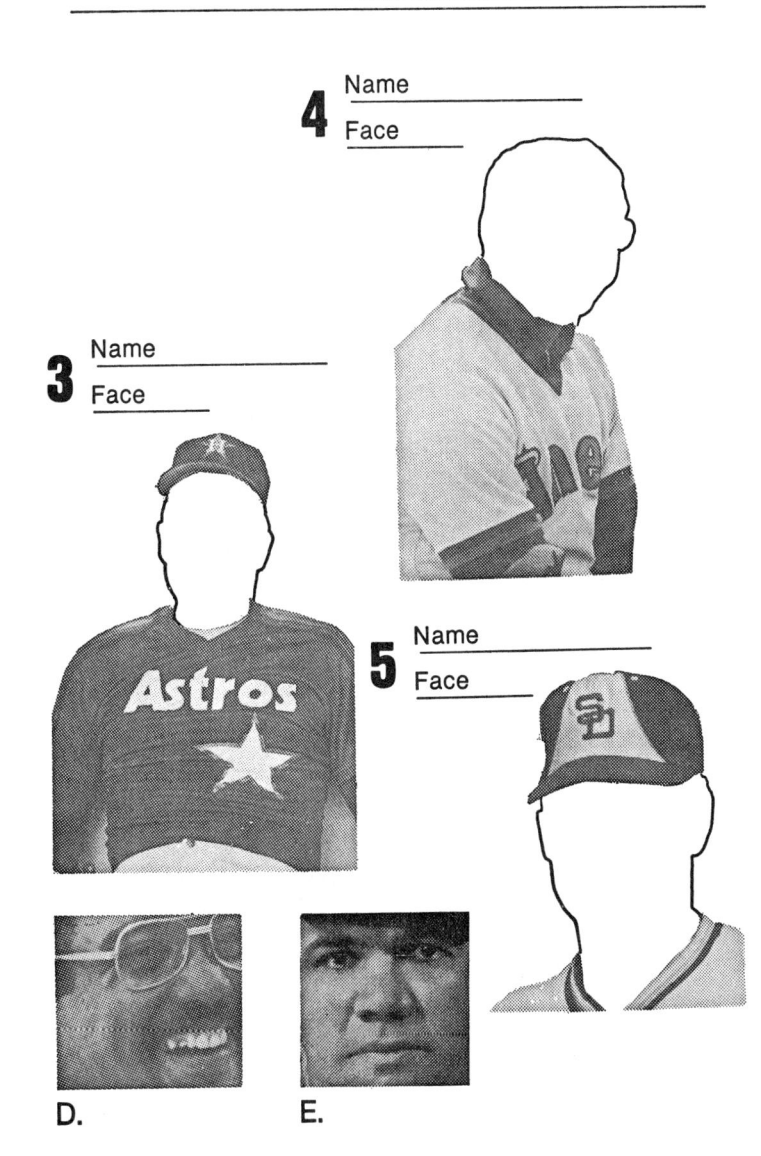

FAMOUS NAME PHOTO GAME 65

4 Name _____
Face ____

3 Name _____
Face ____

5 Name _____
Face ____

D.

E.

66 THE BASEBALL QUIZ BOOK

6 Name _____
Face ____

7 Name _____
Face ____

F.

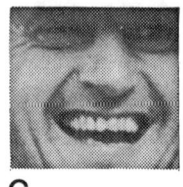

G.

H.

FAMOUS NAME PHOTO GAME 67

9 Name _____
Face _____

8 Name _____
Face _____

10 Name _____
Face _____

I.

J.

68 THE BASEBALL QUIZ BOOK

11 Name
Face

12 Name
Face

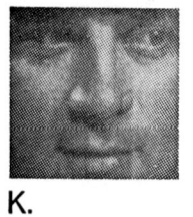

K. 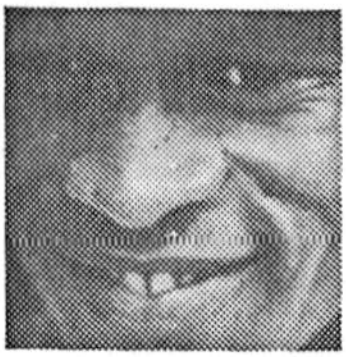   L. 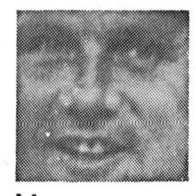   M.

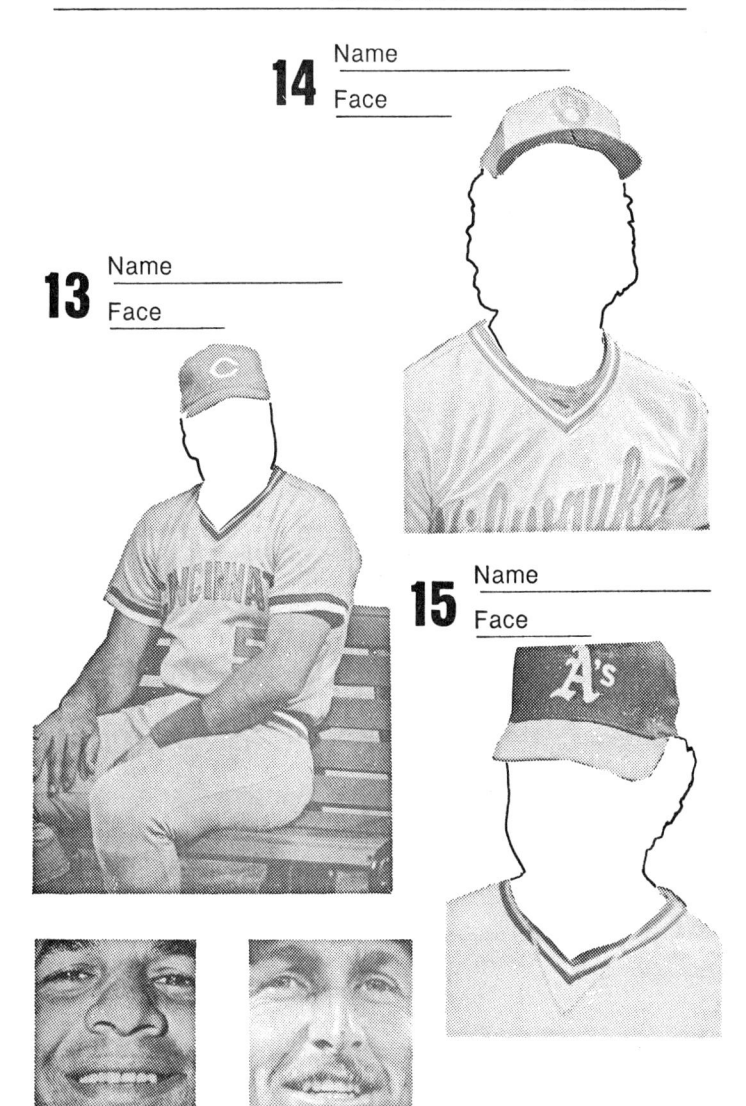

FAMOUS NAME PHOTO GAME 69

14 Name _____
Face _____

13 Name _____
Face _____

15 Name _____
Face _____

N.   O.

Famous Name Photo Game
Answers
1. Babe Ruth (E)
2. Sandy Koufax (A)
3. Nolan Ryan (B)
4. Reggie Jackson (D)
5. Steve Garvey (C)
6. Steve Carlton (I)
7. Carl Yastrzemski (G)
8. Billy Martin (J)
9. Rod Carew (F)
10. Dave Winfield (H)
11. George Brett (M)
12. Roy Campanella (N)
13. Johnny Bench (K)
14. Robin Yount (O)
15. Rickey Henderson (L)

Section III
Answers

Answers

1 **True. True. True. True.** An interesting phenomenon occurred four times since the MVP award has been given out. A change of scenery helped the likes of Roger Maris, who won the MVP in 1960, while with the Yankees after being traded by the Kansas City A's in 1959. Frank Robinson went from the 1965 Reds to win the MVP in 1966 with the Orioles. Richie Allen also turned the trick in 1972 while with the White Sox after being traded by the Dodgers and Bob Elliott in 1947 with the Braves won the MVP after being traded in 1946 from the Pirates.

2 **(C) Willie Mays** won the National League's MVP award in 1954 while playing for the pennant winning New York Giants. 11 years later while playing for the San Francisco Giants Giants and hitting 52 homers, he won the MVP title again.

3 **(C)** The date was September 27, 1951. **Bill Sharman** had just been called up from the minors to sit on the bench of the Dodgers, when the home plate umpire, Frank Dascoli, ejected everyone on the bench from the game for arguing a close play at the plate. Sharman was one of them and never got into a game that season, nor did he make it back afterwards. This is the same Bill Sharman who was one of the all-time basketball greats and is now the President of the Los Angeles Lakers.

4 **Vic Janowicz** was an Ohio State halfback who won the Heisman Trophy in 1950. Vic also played for the Pittsburgh Pirates in 1953 and 1954. His lifetime batting average was .286 after appearing in 83 contests. Janowicz was primarily a catcher but played third and the outfield.

5 **(A)** From 1959-1962, All-Star competition was a two-game affair. In 1959, **Don Drysdale** got the nod to start both games. He lost one and did not figure in the decision of the other.

6 **(A)** Since 1900, the record is **three triple plays** by one club in one season and is shared by four different teams. The most recent of clubs to administer the triple killings three times in one season was the 1965 Chicago Cubs. An interesting note would be the year the last American League club accomplished this unusual feat. It has been more than 50 years since an American League team has executed a triple play three times in one season. The team was the Boston Red Sox in 1924.

ANSWERS 75

7 Believe it or not, the record for most games postponed is **nine**. The team that fell victim to all of the cancellations was the old National League Philadelphia club back in August of 1903. What a headache for the travelling secretary that must have been! Their record was a dismal 49 wins and 86 losses. Maybe it was a blessing in disguise.

8 **(C) Yaz** hit 24 homers in 1979 to lead the pack of 40 year olds. Williams led the group with a .328 average the year he turned 40 while Yaz led in RBIs with 87.

9 **(C)** Probably the greatest of all switch hitters, **Mantle** poked home runs from the right and left sides in the same game **ten** different times. Hall of Famer Mantle first accomplished the feat on May 13, 1955 and last amazed the fans on August 12, 1964.

10 **(A) The Cincinnati club back in 1883** was the first team to use numbers on their uniforms, but the idea was not accepted until the 1929 Yankees initiated the idea in the American League. In other words, Babe Ruth did not have the number 3 on his back the first nine years he played for the Bronx Bombers.

11 **(C) Sal Durante**, a 19-year-old truck driver from Brooklyn, made the catch. Durante turned in the historic home run ball to Sacramento restaurateur Sam Gordon for $5,000.

12 **(B)** The only man to pinch hit for baseball's all-time leading home run hitter was **Mike Lum.** Lum was sent up to the plate to swing for Aaron in 1969.

76 THE BASEBALL QUIZ BOOK

13 (A) Bob L. Miller was the pitcher who won a game for the Mets in 1967, but was traded before he could win another. Twelve years later he was traded back to the Mets and won his second game on April 30, 1974.

14 (C) Many would quickly say it would have to be Hall of Famer Roy Campanella, but the honors belong to **Joe Ferguson**. Joe led the team in 1973 with 25 home runs and 88 RBI.

15 (B) It was the last day of the season when Joe Pignatano was batting against the Cubs in Wrigley Field. In Joe's last at bat, he managed to hit into a **triple play**, thus ending this 1962 season and his career.

16 (C) Hall of Famer Mell Ott of the New York Giants was intentionally passed **five times** in the second game of a doubleheader on Oct. 5, 1929. In the American League the record is held by Roger Maris who got a free pass to first four times in a 12 inning game on May 22, 1962.

17 (B) Who else could hold such a record other than the Bronx Bombers. The **1941 New York Yankees** hit a home run in each game they played for 25 games to set the record. It all began on June 1 and lasted until June 29. The Yanks hit a total of 40 homers during that time span. The home run leaders on the club included Keller (33), DiMaggio (30), and Henrich (31). The Yankees somehow managed to win 101 games that season and finish first.

18 (B) Texas Ranger Manager Doug Rader is the author.

ANSWERS 77

19 True. In 1972, Rod Carew won the American League batting crown with a .318 average that included 170 hits, but not one of them was a home run.

20 (B) Enos Slaughter NY Yanks 56
St. Louis 46
Frank Robinson Baltimore Orioles 70, 71
Cincinnati Reds 61
Roger Maris NY Yanks 60, 61, 62
St. Louis 67
Bill Skowrown NY Yanks 55, 56, 58, 60
L.A. Dodgers 63

21 (D) The record for most errors in one game by two clubs combined is an astounding **40.** The two clubs involved were the National League's Boston and St. Louis teams. That fatal date was June 14, 1876. Boston led the list with 24 erros while St. Louis had only 16 miscues.

22 1. Nolan Ryan (C) Lynn
2. Tom Seaver (D) George
3. Richie Ashburn (F) Don
4. Sparky Lyle (A) Albert
5. Mike Shannon (E) Thomas
6. Dixie Walker (B) Fred

23 (B) Clem Labine went to bat 31 times in 1955 and only got three hits. Ironically, each of those three hits were homers. On the other hand, Labine's 1955 record was 13 wins, 5 losses and 11 saves.

24 (A) The highest slugging average for one season (100 or more games) is held by **Babe Ruth** with a fantastic .847 mark in 1920. That was the year the Sultan of Swat had 172 hits

78 THE BASEBALL QUIZ BOOK

including an unheard of 54 homers, nine triples, and 36 doubles in 458 at-bats.

25 (A) Believe it or not, Gray struck out only **11 times.** He went to bat 234 times and managed 51 hits for a .218 batting average.

26 (B) The record goes to Hall of Famer **Brooks Robinson** who somehow managed it four times. The dates were June 2, 1958, September 10, 1964, August 18, 1965, and August 6, 1967.

27 False. Tony Mullane, who pitched from 1881 to 1894 had a career mark of 285 wins. The Baseball Encyclopedia lists him as BB TB which means Bats Both, Throws Both.

28 (D) In 1967, with a 162 game schedule, the **New York Mets** managed to use a total of 54 players for one season. The outcome was still the same as the Mets finished in the cellar as they had the previous five years. It's no wonder that the Mets had a couple of field managers, namely Wes Westrum and Salty Parker.

29 (C) Casey was referring to marvelous *Marv Throneberry.* An interesting side note though; of the regulars playing the infield, **Throneberry** led the team in fielding average .981. However, Marv's 17 errors led National League first baseman that year.

30 (C) For a nine inning game, the most pitchers used by two teams is **14.** The record has been tied six times. An interesting note — one team, the Houston Astros, figured in the record twice. They first tied it back in 1967 along with the Cubs and then tied it again in 1972 while playing the Dodgers. Both times the Houston club used eight pitchers while the opposition used six.

31 (C) Tris Speaker toed the mound only once for the Boston Red Sox and then hurriedly returned to the outfield after giving up one run on two hits for an ERA of 9.00. As Casey Stengel used to say, "You can look it up."

32 Yup! It is not as uncommon a feat as you would think. There have been seven pitchers to reach the magic number 20 on both the winning and losing side the same season. Among them, the most notable would be Walter Johnson. The Big Train, as he was known, won 25 games in 1916 while losing an even 20 games.

33 (C) 502. Doesn't everyone know that!

34 (D) Everyone knows that the losing pitcher was Dodger hurler **Ralph Branca** who wore number 13. The winning pitcher, who to this day has been almost forgotten, was Larry Jansen whose record was 23-11 in 1951.

35 (D) The game must be a forfeit to the opposing team when such a situation occurs. Under Baseball Rule 4.17: "A game shall be forfeited to the opposing team when a team is unable or refuses to place nine players on the field."

36 (B) Rocky Colavito pitched 2-2/3 innings in relief while with the Yanks in a game in 1978, and was around at the end to get credit for the victory. Rocky also pitched in one game in 1958 for the Indians but did not affect the outcome of the game. **Colavito hit 374 homers,** stole 19 bases and led the American League once in 1959 with 42 round trippers.

37 (D) Jim Bunning won a total of 118 games while pitching in the American League for the Detroit Tigers (1955-63). In the National League, Jim won a total of 106 while pitching for the Phils (64-67, 70-71), Pit (68-69) and LA (69). Jim also pitched a no-hitter in both leagues.

38 Yes. It's a tricky one. The answer is Bill McGowan. McGowan appeared in 2,541 consecutive games, spanning 16½ years from 1925-1954. The question as it is written is correct, for McGowan was an American League umpire and indeed appeared in more games consecutively than Lou Gehrig.

39 Yes. He was a halfback at Louisiana State University in the mid-40's along with Yelberton Abraham Tittle and also was a standout shortstop for 14 years in the National League. His name is Alvin Dark. Dark played from 1946 to 1960 and hit a total of 126 homers, two of them off Hall of Famer Sandy Koufas.

40 No. No one in the major leagues has ever won 20 games in a season without losing. However, way back in 1880, Fredrick Goldsmith of Chicago (NL) came close as he won 22 and lost 3. This achievement was repeated in 1951 by Edwin "Preacher" Roe of Brooklyn (NL) as he won 22 regular season games with 3 losses.

41 Sure. By a forfeit (tricky, huh?).

ANSWERS 81

42 (B) Carl Scheib was a pitcher for the old Philadelphia A's on September 6, 1943. He was 16 years, 8 months and 5 days old. He was 0-1 and had a 4.34 ERA that season. He lasted for eleven years in the majors.

43 (D) Joseph D. Sullivan, while playing shortstop for the National League's Washington club in 1983, holds the all-time errors record in one season. Sullivan played in 127 games that year and managed to be credited with a total of **106 errors.** The sure-handed Sullivan batted .266. It is our opinion that this record of Sullivan's will stand the test of time along with DiMaggio's 56 game hitting streak, Gehrig's consecutive game endurance record and Vander Meer's double no-hitter.

44 (C) Mantle, Maris and Bill Skowron. The 1961 season wound up with Maris hitting 61 homers, Mantle 54, and, to round out the trio, Bill Skowron, the Yankee first baseman also known as "Moose," with 28 for a total of 143. The number two trio was Ruth, Gehrig and Lazzeri in 1927. Their total homers came to 125 with Ruth leading with 60, Gehrig with 47, while Lazzeri collected 18 round-trippers.

45 (C) Big Dave Winfield was born in St. Paul, Minesota on Oct. 3, 1951, the same day that Bobby Thomson hit his playoff homer that clinched the pennant for the New York Giants from the Brooklyn Dodgers.

46 (A) Timewise, the Giants took care of the Phils in 1919 one September afternoon in **51 minutes** by a score of 6-1.

47 (B) Bob Shaw of the 1963 Milwaukee Braves

holds the record for balking in one season with **eight balks.** The record was tied in 1974 by Bill Bonham of the Cubs. An interesting note is the fact that Shaw also holds the record for most balks in one game, five, which probably accounts for the fact that he also led the league the same year.

48 (C) Hall of Famer Lou Boudreau was appointed manager of the Cleveland Indians November 25, 1941 at the **age of 24 years, 4 months, 8 days.** But technically, the record belongs to Roger Peckinpaugh who was appointed manager of the Yankees on Sept. 16, 1914 at the age of 23 years, 7 months, 11 days.

49 (C) **White Sox catcher Ray Schalk.** Schalk, whose career spanned from 1912 to 1929 while playing in 1,760 games, managed a lifetime batting average of .253. Schalk's best season with the bat was in 1919 when he averaged .282. The other Hall of Famers lifetime batting averages are: Tommy McCarthy .292, Johnny Evers .270, Bobby Wallace .268.

50 (C) **The St. Louis Browns** run away with the record for most runners left on base with a total of 1,334. The Browns accomplished this dubious record in 1941 while finishing sixth in an eight team league and had a combined team batting averag of .266. Over in the National League, the record is held by the 1969 Giants who left 1,280 men stranded on base.

51 (C) **Honus P. Wagner,** Pittsburgh's Hall of Famer, won the batting title in 1911 at the age of 37 years, 231 days. Honus hit .344 while playing shortstop for the Bucs which was above his lifetime batting average of .328. In 1958, Ted Williams of the American League Red Sox was 40 when he set the major league record for winning the batting title late in his career with an average of .328.

52 (B) The Milwaukee Braves had **four consecutive homers** by Eddie Mathews, Hank Aaron, Joe Adcock and Frank Thomas, when they played the Reds on June 8, 1961. The Brave slug-fest took place in the seventh inning of the game. Eddie Mathews hit 32 homers that season, while Aaron had 34, Thomas 25, and Adcock 35.

53 True. Its happened a couple of times. Bobo Newson while pitching for the St. Louis Browns in 1938, had a record of 20-16 with an ERA of 5.08. And in 1930 Remy Kremer of the Pirates won 20, lost 12, and had a 5.02 ERA.

54 (D) The record for an American League team is held by the 1921 **Detroit Tigers** who batted .316, which included Ty Cobb's .389 and league-leading Harry Heilman's .394. In the National League, the **Phillies** had a team batting average of .343 in 1894. Four of the Phillies batted over .400. The team was lead by Tuck Turner, an outfielder who hit .416. Interestingly enough, Turner whose career began in 1893, no longer played major league ball after the 1898 season and finished with a lifetime .320 season.

55 (D) The player who replaced "The Iron Horse" at his position was none other than **Ellsworth "Babe" Dahlgren,** in 1938. Dahlgren's career spanned from 1935-1946. Playing for eight

84 THE BASEBALL QUIZ BOOK

major league clubs, he played in a total of 1,137 games compiling a lifetime average of .261.

56 **The score would be 3 to 1** due to the fact that the hit was a ground rule double, the hitter gets credit with a double driving in two runs. The only time a situation occurs like this is when the batter hits either a home run or a ground rule double. To get full credit, the correct amount of runs due to the force must be counted. In the same situation, if the player had hit what looked like a double down the line, he would then only be credited with a single which is all it would take to get the runner in from third and win the game. They key word is "automatic" in this case such as ground rule double and home run.

57 **(D) Bob Lemon,** the pitcher, was playing center that historic day, as he always wanted to play in the outfield and had the ability and bat to do so. Lem played in the outfield 12 times that season and two more times the following year. Bob, whose lifetime batting average was .232, also played a couple of games at third base early in his career.

58 **(A)** The very tired and hard luck umpire named **Ed Sudol.** Ed played minor league baseball as a first baseman beginning in 1940 through 1953. Sudol then started his umpiring career and made the majors in 1957.

59 **(C) John McGraw** in 1899 managed the Baltimore Orioles in the National League while playing third base. Baltimore finished in fourth place, while winning 86 and losing 62.

ANSWERS 85

60 (D) The fact that Dave Bancroft had the habit of shouting **"Beauty"** on each good pitch to the opposition while in the minors led to his nickname. Bancroft played short for the Phillies and Giants and once had six singles in six at-bats on June 28, 1920.

61 (A) Since 1900, the record for most runs scored in a single inning is held by the old **Brooklyn Dodgers.** They scored 15 runs in the first inning of a game against the Reds on May 21, 1952. Team members included Gil Hodges, Jackie Robinson, Duke Snider, Roy Campanella and Carl Furillo.

62 True. Dom DiMaggio won the title with only 15 thefts. Phil Rizzuto of the Yankees and Elmer Valo of Philadelphia tied for the number two spot with twelve steals each. Obviously, either the catchers had great arms or the running game was not a big part of baseball at that time.

63 (B) The Yankees come up short at second base for the Hall of Fame.

	Yanks	Cubs	Giants
1st Base	Lou Gehrig Johnny Mize	Frank Chance Ernie Banks Cap Anson	Bill Terry
2nd Base		Billy Herman Rogers Hornsby Johnny Evers	Frank Frisch
Shortstop	Joe Sewell	Joe Tinker	Travis Jackson Dave Bancroft
3rd Base	Frank Baker	Fred Lindstrom	Fred Lindstrom
Outfield	Willie Keeler Joe DiMaggio	Kiki Cuyler Hack Wilson	Willie Mays

Out- field	Mickey Mantle Earl Combes Babe Ruth	King Kelly Chuck Klein	Ross Youngs Mel Ott

Pitcher	Whitey Ford
	Lefty Gomez
	Red Ruffing
	Jack Chesbro
	Waite Hoyt
	Herb Pennock
		Mordecai
		  Brown
		Dizzy Dean
		Burleigh
		  Grimes
		Grover
		  Alexander
			Carl Hubbell
			Rube Marquart
			Christy
			  Mathewson
			Joe McGinnity

Catcher	Yogi Berra
	Bill Dickey
		Gabby
		  Hartnett
			Roger
			  Bresnahan

64 (B) Not as highly publicized as home runs but just as rare, if not more so, is the player who hits the most triples in one game. This feat has been accomplished in the American League 15 times with the record of **three triples.** Over in the National League, the record is **four** with only one player laying claim to it. He is William Joyce of the 1897 Giants on May 18th.

65 (C) Augie Galan of the Chicago Cubs was the first player to hit homers from both sides of the plate in one game on June 25, 1937. Augie hit a total of 18 homers that year and finished his career with a grand total of 100 in 16 years of playing time.

66 (C) The record for hits in one season (excluding 1887 when a walk was counted as a hit) belongs to Hall of Famer **George Sisler** who collected 257 hits in the 1920 campaign while playing for St. Louis. Sisler hit .407 that year.

67 (A) The major league record for a team being shut out over one season belongs to the **St. Louis Cardinals**. The Cards managed to lose 33 games in the 1908 season without scoring

ANSWERS 87

one run. The 1909 Senators hold the American League record for being shut out in 29 games in one year.

68 (D) The first player to hit a home run during a night game was **Floyd "Babe" Herman** on July 10, 1935 while playing for Cincinnati. Babe ended a very distinguished twenty year career in baseball spanning from 1926-1945 and finishing with a lifetime batting average of .323.

69 (C) On July 10, 1932, John H. Burnett, a second baseman and shortstop for the Cleveland Indians, appeared at the plate 11 times during an 18-inning game. During this marathon, Burnett collected **nine** base hits, two of which were doubles. A number of players have since come close to this record with many having seven hits in a single game. Rennie Stennett of the Pittsburgh Pirates set a major league record of seven consecutive hits in one game on September 16, 1975 against the Chicago Cubs.

70 (B) The records reveal that the old **Philadelphia A's of 1949** led both leagues in double plays with a record that still stands at 217. It's interesting to note that they did this during the days of a 154 game schedule. That twin killing combination included Eddie Joost at short, Pete Suder at 2nd, and Ferris Fain at 1st (doesn't sound as good as Tinkers to Evers to Chance, but they got the job done.)

71 (C) The San Francisco Giants played the Mets on May 31, 1964 and didn't complete it until June 1. The time was **seven hours, twenty-three minutes** (23 innings). Ironically it was the second game of a doubleheader. The Giants won the contest by a score of 8 to 6.

88 THE BASEBALL QUIZ BOOK

The American League record is 7 hours when the Yanks and Tigers went at it for 22 innings on June 24, 1962. The Yankees emerged as victors by a score of 9 to 7.

72 (D) Billy Martin.

73 No. The umpire who calls the infield fly rule will also say at the same time, while the ball is in the air, that the batter is out only if the ball is in fair territory. The infield fly rule is to prevent a player from dropping the ball on purpose and getting two easy outs. If the ball is in foul territory and the player drops it, it is just a foul ball and no one is forced to run.

74 (B) According to the Sporting News record book, the record listing for the man who has thrown the greatest distance belongs to **Glen E. Gorbous.** The record was set in Omaha, Nebraska on August 1, 1957. Glen threw a regulation baseball a total distance of 445 feet, 10 inches on the fly.

75 (B) The honor for hitting into the most double plays in a season goes to Boston Red Sox star **Jackie Jensen.** The year was 1954 when Jensen hit into 32 twin killings. An interesting aside, the lifetime record for grounding into the most double plays belongs to Hank Aaron who has the lifetime mark of .328 but never led the league in a season.

76 (A) Lee May connected while playing for the Reds when Tom Terrific broke in on April 30, 1967 at Cincinnati. He ended the season with a 16-13 mark.

77 1.   Gene Conley   (E) Donald

ANSWERS

2.	Sherm Lollar	(C)	John
3.	Cookie Lavagetto	(A)	Harry
4.	Mickey Owen	(B)	Arnold
5.	Randy Hundley	(F)	Cecil
6.	Lee May	(D)	Arthur

78 **(C) Phil Cavarretta** started his career in 1934 with the Chicago Cubs and ended it in 1955 with the Chicago White Sox.

79 **Yes,** but not in the same year. Brooklyn Dodger great, Don Newcombe won the Rookie of the Year award in 1949 when he posted a 17-8 record. In 1956, he won both the Cy Young award and National League's Most Valuable Player honors with a record of 27-7.

80 **(B) 1/8.** The 37" midget appeared as a pinch hitter for the St. Louis Browns in 1951 and walked. Eddie was hitting for Eddie Sawyer.

81 **(D)** Sounds crazy, but in 1960 **Whitey Herzog,** while playing for the Kansas City A's against the Washington Senators, managed to do it. Camilio Pascual was pitching and Herzog lined one back to him, who then threw to Julio Becquerto, who then threw to Jose Valdivielso thus completing the first all Cuban triple play.

82 **(B)** No, it's not Satchel Paige. Although he faced both, Paige was not in the majors when he worked against Ruth. The pitcher's name was **Al Benton.** Benton started his career in 1934 and finished up in 1952. His final career statistics are 98-88 with a 3.66 ERA.

83 **Tony Oliva** hit one out as a DH on opening day for the Twins on April 4, 1973.

84 **(B) Three,** the record was set in 1883 when

three different players accomplished this amazing feat, all in the same game for the Cubs on September 6. The only other player to get three hits in one inning was Gene Stephens while playing for the Boston Red Sox on June 18, 1953. Stephens collected two singles and one double in the seventh inning.

85 (D) Hardrock.

86 (B) The record for a nine-inning contest goes to a game between the San Diego Padres and the Cincinnati Reds back on September 15, 1972 when the total strikeouts were **28.**

87 (D) In doubleheaders on June 19 and June 21, 1983, Mike "Pinky" Higgins of the Boston Red Sox collected twelve consecutive hits, plus two walks, thus reaching base a record **14** straight times. Pinky's lifetime batting average was .292 in 14 years as a major leaguer.

88 Yes. 13 players in baseball history have played for 3 different teams in World Series competition. Among the more recent players to accomplish this feat were Eddie Stanky while with the 1947 Dodgers, 1948 Braves and 1951 Giants. Andy Pafko turned the trick while with the 1945 Cubs, 1952 Dodgers and the 1957-58 Milwaukee Braves.

89 (D) Ron Santo of the Cubs said no and exercised a new baseball rule concerning trades of players with ten years time and five years of tenure with the same team. The Cubs wanted to trade him to the California Angels, but Ron said no and decided to move across town to the White Sox instead.

ANSWERS 91

90 (C) Joe DeMaestri finished the inning for the injured Kubek. However, regular third baseman Clete Boyer took over the next inning and veteran infielder Gil McDougald handled the chores at third.

91 Yes. Not as common as one would think; 100 plus RBI men are usually your home run hitters but there have been a handful of exceptions to the rule. Among them is Willie Montanez who, in 1975, hit 10 homers and had 101 runs batted in. Wes Parker, in 1970, had 111 RBI while hitting only 10 homers. Dixie Walker's 1946 stats read 9 homers, 116 RBI to name just a few.

92 (C) Larry Dierker in 1969 had a 20-13 record while seeing action in 39 games and having a 2.33 ERA.

93 (B) Bobby Bonds against the Dodgers on June 25, 1968, his first major league game, hit a grandslam. Bonds added eight more homers to his credit that season for a total of nine.

94 (A) Since 1900, the record is **four** different teams and is held by many players. The most recent player to call four different towns home in one season is Dave Kingman in 1977. Kingman played for the Mets, Padres, Angels and Yankees.

95 (C) Boston Red Sox slugger Jim Rice has passed the 20 total in every department except for triples during his career. The following is the list of the other players and the year in which they accomplished the feat. Jim Bottomley 1928; Willie Mays 1957; and George Brett 1979.

96 (B) Fred Clarke collected **five** safeties for Louisville of the National League in 1894 in his first game on June 30th. Clarke finished the season batting .275. Since 1900, the record is four hits and is held by Casey Stengel, Willie McCovey and Mack Jones.

97 (B) Would you believe that **Sal "The Barber" Maglie** figures in on both games as the other pitcher. In 1951, Maglie started the game and went the first eight innings only to have Larry Jansen come in to pitch the ninth and get the victory. In 1956, it was Maglie again who took the other role in baseball history as he was Don Larsen's match-up in the fifth game of the World Series.

98 (D) After pitching no-hitters on June 11 and June 15, Vander Meer faced the Boston Bees on June 19. He threw **three and one-third innings of hitless ball.** The player to break the no-hit spell was third baseman Deb Garms with a line single to short left-center that day in 1938.

99 (C) Spanning two seasons, **Carl Hubbell** of the New York Giants won 24 games. King Carl's streak started on July 17, 1936 and lasted until May 27, 1937. The screwball King won his last 16 games in 1936 and won his first eight games of the 1937 season.

100 (C) Hank Aaron (See chart below)
1961 Maris — 61 home runs, 67 strikeouts
1927 Ruth — 60 home runs, 89 strikeouts
1971 Aaron — 47 home runs, 58 strikeouts
1965 Mays — 52 home runs, 71 strikeouts

101 (B) William H. White who played for Boston in the National League in 1877.

ANSWERS 93

102 (A,B,C) They all did except for Lou Brock. The feat of getting more walks than hits is unusual but not rare. Eddie Stanky (The Brat) did it three times in his career while Ted Williams did it once in 1954 with 136 bases on balls and only 133 hits. And Jimmy Wynn did it in 1969 with 148 bases on balls and 133 hits.

103 (B) Babe Ruth never hit a single, double, triple, and homer in one game. The record for hitting the cycle is three, by two players, Bob Meusel of the 1920's Yankees and Babe Herman while with the Cubs and Dodgers in the 1930's. Brock accomplished his "cycle" against the Padres in the mid '70's.

104 (A) .3489 Chick Hafey, St. Louis; **(B)** .3486 Bill Terry, New York; **(C)** .3482 Jim Bottomley, St. Louis; **(D)** .337 Chuck Klein.

105 (D) Hall of Famer Bob Lemon went in to finish the mound duties after Score was carried from the field. Lemon got the win for the Indians while Tom Sturdivant took the loss for the New York Yankees.

106 (C) There have been fourteen left-handed catchers. Jack Clements, of course, heads the list with over 1,000 games caught to his credit. The last left-hander to try working behind the plate was Dale Long who caught for the Cubs in a couple of games back in 1958.

107 Lefty Phillips piloted the Angels from 1969-1971, **Danny Ozark** has been the skipper of the Philadelphia Phillies since 1973, and **Preston Gomez** managed the Padres from 1969-1972 and was also the manager of the Houston Astros from 1974-1975.

108 (C) Bruno Hess walked 16 batters in a game played in 1915. It was Hess' first game in the majors, coincidentally.

109 (D) The year was 1980 when the White Sox only managed to hit a total of **three** homers as a team in one season. (Talk about the dead ball.)

110 (B) It wasn't too long ago when the record for team strikeouts was set by the **1968 San Francisco Giants.** That season the Giants managed to strike out 1,203 times. Bobby Bonds was in his first season and played in only 81 games, but still managed to lead his club in strikeouts with 84. Other players who were up there in "K's" were Willie Mays with 81, Willie McCovey with 71, and Dick Dietz with 68.

111 (B) Joe Gordon hit in 29 consecutive games in 1942 while playing 2nd base for the Yankees. That 29 game streak is also held by Roger Peckinpaugh in 1919 and Earl Combs in 1931. Gordon had a season average that year of .318 as compared to DiMaggio's 1941 .357 average.

112 (B) The National League record is held by the Washington club which played in 1888. The total combined batting average for that club was **.207.** It is no wonder that they finished in last place and were led in hitting by Dummy Hoy with .274. In the American League, the lowest team batting average belongs to the 1910 Chicago White Sox who hit a robust .212. Surprisingly, they finished sixth in an eight-team league and were led in hitting by Patsy Dougherty, an outfielder who hit .248.

113 Yes. Sounds unlikely, but there are two players who were involved in a triple play

ANSWERS 95

twice in one season. Wilbur Cooper, a pitcher for the Pirates in 1922 was involved on July 7 and August 22. The other player was Charlie Jamieson, a Cleveland outfielder who was involved in two triple plays, one on May 23 and the other on June 9, 1928.

114 **(B)** The record is a lucky **seven for seven.** The first time a player went to bat seven times and came up with seven hits was back on June 10, 1892. The player was Wilbert Robinson and he was then playing for the old Baltimore Orioles club. The only player to tie it was Rennie Stennett of the Pirates. Stennett accomplished this rare feat not too long ago on September 16, 1975.

115 **(A)** The total no-hitters by one pitcher in the same season would be two and it has been done by **five** different pitchers. The most famous of all the two no-hitters in one season has to be Johnny Vandermeer's two games in 1938. Not only were they in the same season, but they were consecutive. Other pitchers with two no-hitters are Jim Maloney in 1965, Allie Reynolds in 1951, Virgil Trucks in 1952, and Nolan Ryan in 1973.

116 **(C) Wes Ferrell** had the most home runs for a pitcher lifetime. He hit 37 round-trippers. Ferrell played from 1927-1941. The teams he played for included Cleveland, Boston, New York, and a brief stint with the old Brooklyn Dodgers. His record as a pitcher was 193-128.

117 **(C) Catfish Hunter** has a lifetime won/loss record in World Series play of five wins and three losses. Hunter's World Series ERA is 3.29 for the 12 games he pitched in.

96 THE BASEBALL QUIZ BOOK

118 (A) The gentlemen all managed major league baseball, some prior to the turn of the century and a few before 1925.

119 (B) The major league record for the most runs scored would be **29**. This number has been reached twice in the history of baseball. The first team to score 29 runs was the Red Sox, vs. Browns on June 8, 1950. It was tied on April 23, 1955 when the White Sox did it against the Kansas City A's. The National League record is 28 runs by the St. Louis Cards on July 6, 1929 in the second game of a doubleheader against the Phillies.

120 (B) The record was set by the **1965 Baltimore Orioles** who committed only 95 errors as a team. It is interesting that Luis Apparicio and Brooks Robinson led the team in most errors with 15 and 14 respectively.

121 (A) It was none other than **Hall of Famer Mel Ott.** While with the Giants, Ott managed to finish second in the seasonal home run derby a record eight times. Ott's runner-up years were 1929, 1931, 1932, 1935, 1939, 1941, 1943 and 1944. Other famous home run runner-ups were Lou Gehrig who had three years as second best and Ted Williams and Hank Aaron who each finished number two four times.

122 (A) The record for most assists by an outfielder for a season belongs to **Chuck Klein** who had 44 in 1930 while playing for the Phils. The single game record is four assists and has been tied ten times. The first time the record was set by Harry Schafer of the Boston Braves on September 26, 1877. The last time was on April 27, 1931 by Boston's Wally Berger.

ANSWERS 97

123 Yes, it's true, a player once stole first base. His name was Germany Schaefer and he played second base for the Washington Senators in 1911 when he pulled the unheard of stunt of stealing first base. What happened was simple; Schaefer went back towards first, after stealing second base, much to the disbelief of his teammates and the opposition. On the next pitch, he again stole second. When asked after the game why he did it, he explained that there was no rule that said he couldn't and he thought it would shake up the visiting team. The next day the rules committee held an emergency meeting and added a new rule prohibiting a player from stealing first base.

124 (A) The World Series of 1905. Every game resulted in a shutout. The two clubs participating were the New York Giants and Philadelphia A's. The Giants won the series by winning four and dropping one, but in each game they played, they either shutout the A's or, for the one game they lost, they themselves were blanked. An interesting note would be the composite batting averages for the teams in that World Series. The World Champion Giants hit .209 collectively while the A's managed to bat .161.

125 (C) Jim Gilliam coached for the Los Angeles Dodgers in the late 60's and was the first black to coach in the National League.

126 (B) Stan Musial led the National League in batting average with .376 and RBI with 131, but came up one short in the home run department with 39 while Johnny Mize and Ralph Kiner each had 40.

127 **(C)** The major league record for assists by a catcher is **214.** It is held by Pat Moran of the old National League Boston club back in 1903. Moran played in 107 games when setting his record but could only brag about his assist record that year as there was not one winning pitcher on the club. The American League record is held by Oscar Stanage with 212 assists. Stanage played for the Tigers in 1911 when he set the record and played in 141 games.

128 **Yes.** The most recent was the 1974 Oakland A's team. Joe Rudi was the club's batting leader and he finished up with .293 that season.

129 **(B)** The date was August 3, 1960 when unofficially, **the Detroit Tigers and Cleveland Indians** swapped managers. Jimmy Dykes, the Tiger manager, switched jobs with Indian skipper, Joe Gordon. Dykes had a record of 44-52 at Detroit and left the club in sixth place. Gordon was 49-46 with Cleveland being in fourth place. Interestingly enough the change did not alter the standings of the two clubs involved prior to the switch.

130 **Yes.** The Chicago Cubs had tried everything to win, back in the early 1960's, and even went as far as not appointing a manager but instead had a "college of coaches" or a "rotating manager." The experiment lasted from 1961 until 1965.

131 **(A) Mickey Mantle** hit the first homer in the Dome during an exhibition game. The first competition homer to be hit there goes to Richie Allen of the Phillies.

132 (D) The National League's John H. Coleman lost a total of **48 games** for Philadelphia back in 1883. His record was 11-48 for a .186 average.

133 (B) Known as a baseball marathon would be the game played on May 1, 1920. The two teams involved were the Brooklyn Dodgers and the Boston Braves. Total innings played was an unbelievable **26.** The game started, according to the **Boston Globe,** at 3:00 p.m. and ended shortly before 7:00 p.m. The remarkable aspect of the game is the fact that both pitchers, Joe Oescher and Leon Cadore went the entire distance but could only come up with a tie score of one to one.

134 (D) In 1903, the Pittsburgh Pirates went through **56 consecutive innings** from June 1 to June 9 without giving up a run to set the record. That scoreless streak included six shutouts. In the American League, the Baltimore Orioles of 1974 recorded a string of 54 scoreless innings to make it into the record books.

135 (B) The Senators' first baseman, Joe Kuhel, hit the only homer for the Washington team while playing in Griffith Stadium for the entire 1945 season. The ironic part of the homer was that it was an inside the park job.

136 (A) You have to go all the way back to the 1879 season to get the answer; one would find **William White** of the Cincinnati team pitching 683 innings. Upon close examination,

White was the only pitcher Cincy had that year so he had all the work he could handle. His record was 43-31 while pitching in 76 games and had an ERA of 1.99. Ed Walsh of the 1908 White Sox has got the American League record with 464 innings. Since 1900, in the National League, the work horse would be Iron Man Joe McGinnity of the Giants in 1903.

137 **(C)** The most homers hit in one season on the road against one club is ten. The record was set by Hall of Famer **Harry Heilman** when Detroit played in Phillie's Shibe Park in the 1922 season. The right-handed hitting Heilman hit 21 homers that year while batting .356. In the National League, Joe Adcock, while playing for the Braves in 1954, hit 9 homers in Ebbets Field and then was tied the next year by Willie Mays of the Giants in the same park.

138 **(A) Yes,** in 1921, the **Babe** was the Yankees regular left fielder and he hit 59 homers to lead all major league lifetime left fielders in one season. Ruth managed to drive in 171 runs while batting .378. The Babe was switched to right field in 1923.

139 Yes. Baseball is known for its records — and postponed games are among the most trivial — but there is a record for them. The Philadelphia Phillies somehow had a total of nine games postponed consecutively in the 1903 season. It must have been the rainy season from August 10-19, 1903.

140 **(A)** There have been three first basemen who, believe it or not, had not one single chance offered in a nine-inning game. The players to practically have the day off were John Clancy of the Chicago White Sox in 1930, Jim Collins with the Chicago Cubs in 1937 and Gene Tenace with the Oakland A's on September 1, 1974.

141 (C) Sam McDowell, known in his hey day as "Sudden Sam," had the best strikeout rate per nine innings for one season. The year was 1965 when the lefthander was playing for the Cleveland Indians. McDowell's average for strikeouts that year was 10.72 for every nine innings pitched. McDowell totaled 325 K's while throwing 273 innings and appearing in 42 games.

142 (B) The record was broken in 1922. It had belonged to Sam Thompson who had a career total of **126 homers.**

143 Yes. Although not strictly enforced by umpires nowadays, the rule reads: "When the bases are unoccupied, the pitcher shall deliver the ball to the batter within 20 seconds after he receives the ball." A violation of this rule would credit the batter with a ball. There have been unsuccessful attempts to construct running clocks to keep time on the pitcher, the last one being in old Municipal Stadium in Kansas City in the mid 1960's.

144 (D) The record is **30** and has been tied four times. The first record-setting left on base mark was accomplished in the National League in 1893 when the Brooklyn club left 16 men on and the Pittsburgh club left 14 men stranded. The last time the record was tied occurred on July 21, 1961 when the Los Angeles Angels and Washington Senators each left 15 men on base for a record tying 30.

145 True. Who else could accomplish such a feat but Hank Aaron? The Hammer is the only player to clout an even 40 homers in only 392 at-bats in 1973.

146 (C) The lowest average to take the league title happened in 1968 when Carl Yazstremski hit .301. In 1902, the home run title belonged to Tom Leach of the Pirates who led his league with only six round-trippers. And the fewest RBI to lead a league goes to Chicago Cub Fred Merkle. Merkle, in 1918 managed only 71 that year.

147 (D) Ed Coleman of the 1936 St. Louis Browns, in his last year in the majors, was the first pinch hitter to get 20 safeties in a season. Normally an outfielder, Ed Coleman went in to pinch hit 62 times during the 1936 campaign and came up with 20 base hits.

148 (A) Ty Cobb tried his luck at pitching twice in 1918 and then once again in 1925.

149 True. Bob Feller started off the 1940 season with a no-hitter against the Chicago White Sox. To end the season on a high note, Angel fireballer, Nolan Ryan threw a no-hitter against the Twins on September 28, 1974, the last game of the season.

150 (B) Joe D. did it twice, and back-to-back no less. In 1939, Joe hit .381 and then the following year slumped to .352, but it was still good enough to lead the league. The other Yanks listed won only one batting average title during their careers.

ANSWERS 103

151 (B) The game is over. According to the official playing rules, the pitch would be declared a **strike.** The definition of a strike is: "a legal pitch when so called by the umpire, which touches the batter as he strikes at it, or touches the batter in flight in the strike zone."

152 (D) National League pitchers have done it **eight times** with Joe Nuxhall, Bob Gibson, Don Drysdale among them. The American League has done it five times with Walter Johnson, Ryan Duren and Mike Cuellar among those select few.

153 (D) The season record for stealing home is a tie between **Pete Reiser** and **Rod Carew.** Both players totalled seven steals of the plate. Reiser set the mark while playing for the Dodgers in 1946 and Carew tied it in 1969 for the Twins. Ty Cobb has the all-time record for stealing home in a career with the amazing total of 35 thefts.

154 (A) The single club record for a nine inning contest is nine pitchers used by St. Louis against the Cubs on October 2, 1949. The record for two clubs would be a total of 14 pitchers which has been reached five times in the history of the game.

155 (B) The answer is **two** and it has been reached six times. The last player to tie the record was Richie Allen while playing for the White Sox. The year was 1972 and the Sox were playing the Twins.

156 (C) The Babe was pulled for a pinch hitter several times. The first was probably the most interesting. The pinch hitter was **Duffy Lewis.**

104 THE BASEBALL QUIZ BOOK

He hit for Ruth in the first game Babe ever pitched, July 11, 1914, in Boston. Lewis got a seventh-inning single that became the winning run in Ruth's 4-3 victory over Cleveland.

157 (C) Brooklyn was playing the Cubs on June 17, 1915 when, with two out in the first inning, George W. Zabel came in to relieve the Cubs' starting pitcher. Zabel continued in the game which lasted a total of 19 innings and got credit for a 4-3 win over the Dodgers. It was Zabel's **18-1/3 innings** of relief work that set the record for a single game.

158 Yes. Believe it or not, Napoleon Lajoie was intentionally walked on May 23, 1901 in the ninth inning with the bases loaded.

159 (C) Harry M. Gowdy of the Boston Braves entered the service on June 27, 1917 to become the first player in World War I.

160 (D) Ray Chapman holds the major league record for sacrifice hits in one season with a total of **67** when he was with Cleveland and played in 156 games during the 1917 campaign.

161 Yes. Since the advent of the lively ball, there has been only one player to take the honors of being the home run king in his league and still strike out less than ten times. The player was Tommy Holmes back in 1945. Holmes led the National League, while playing for the Boston Braves, with a total of 28 round-trippers with the amazing statistic of striking out only nine times.

162 (C) The Cleveland Indians were playing the White Sox on September 20, 1905 when in the

ANSWERS 105

eighth inning the Indians managed a total of **seven errors** for the major league record. As for the National League record, it is held by the Pittsburgh Pirates with six errors.

163 (A) Joe Black of the Brooklyn Dodgers beat the Yankees on October 1, 1952 in the opening game of the World Series by a score of 4-2 at Ebbets Field.

164 (C) The major league record for hits in a single 9-inning contest goes to a game played on August 17, 1894. Philadelphia played Louisville and had a slugfest with a **36** hit attack for the Philadelphia club.

165 (B) The Boston club of the National League committed **24** miscues when playing St. Louis on June 14, 1876 to win the honors of the worst single game fielding effort by a team.

166 Yes. The World Series happened to be the 1903 series which was the best of nine instead of the best of seven as we know today. The Pirates played the Red Sox, Pittsburgh lost the Series as Deacon Phillippe won three games for the National League club, while Bill Dineen won three games and Cy Young won two contests teaming up to win it for Boston.

167 (B) Jackie Jensen stole 22 bases for the Red Sox of the American League in 1954.

168 Yes. Bob Nieman of the St. Louis Browns started his career off with a bang on September 14, 1951 when he hit a home run in his first two major league at-bats. Nieman totalled 125 homers in his career that lasted **12** years with five different teams.

106 THE BASEBALL QUIZ BOOK

169 (D) In **1974**, umpires were given permission to wear eyeglasses if these were needed (no joke folks).

170 (C) There have been **eight** unassisted triple plays in the history of baseball. The first happened on July 19, 1907 by Neal Ball, a shortstop for the Cleveland Indians against the Red Sox. Ron Hansen was the last player to pull an unassisted triple killing. It happened while he was playing for the Senators against Cleveland on July 30, 1968. Both Ball and Hansen caught a line drive with men on first and second and stepped on second base to double-up the man on second and tag the runner coming in from first.

171 (C) The 1936 Yankees lead all teams in RBI for a season with 995. Five players had more than 100 RBI's. They were George Selkirk and Bill Dickey with 107 each, Tony Lazzeri with 109, Joe DiMaggio with 125 and Lou Gehrig leading the club with 152 RBI's.

172 (D) If you answered Lou Gehrig you're wrong. The answer is **Jake Beckley** who played for the Pittsburgh, Cincinnati and St. Louis clubs of the National League from 1888-1907. "Eagle Eye" as he was known, played in 2,386 games for the number one spot, while Mickey Vernon played in 2,237 games for second place and Lou Gehrig played in 2,136 games for third place.

173 (B) The player is none other than The Man! **Stan "The Man" Musial's** career spanned from 1941-1963 with the St. Louis Cards. Musial was inducted into baseball's Hall of Fame in 1969. Also added to Musial's impressive stats would be his 475 homers and 1,951 RBI, not to mention 3,630 hits!

174 **(A)** The American League record for consecutive extra inning ball games is **five** and it belongs to the 1908 Detroit Tigers. The Tigers had the misfortune of being involved in extra inning games from September 9-13, 1908. Over in the National League, the record is four extra inning games and the team involved was the 1917 Pittsburgh Pirates from August 18-22.

175 **(D)** The season record since 1900 belongs to **Chuck Klien** of the 1930 Philadelphia club with 44 outfield assists. As for lifetime, the record belongs to Hall of Famer **Tris Speaker** with 450 over a span of 22 years.

176 **(C) Jim Bagby,** while with the Cleveland Indians homered in the 1920 World Series on October 10 to become the first pitcher to hold that distinction. The unfortunate pitcher on the other end of that homer was Burleigh Grimes, now a Hall of Famer, when he played with the Brooklyn Dodgers.

177 False. It's .450. Ted Williams got the pitching ambition off his chest with a 1940 one-time performance. He pitched two innings, striking out one batter.

178 Yes. It has happened more than once in the majors, but the first man to hit that first delivery for a home run was Eddie Morgan of the St. Louis Cards back on April 14, 1936. An interesting note would be the fact that it was the only homer of his career. Morgan's career lasted but 65 more official at-bats.

108 THE BASEBALL QUIZ BOOK

179 **(A)** Hammerin' Hank had **488** home runs after he reached 8,399 career at-bats in May 1968.

180 **(C) Honus Wagner.** An interesting side note is that King Kelly played every position except for pitcher.

181 **(B) Stan "The Man" Musial** tried his luck at pitching in the majors in that 1952 game after having been converted from a pitcher to a fielder in the minors years earlier.

182 **(A) Zero.** Amazingly, in Perry's long career he never led the league in strikeouts. His best year was 1973 when he pitched for Cleveland and struck out 238 batters; that just happens to be the year Nolan Ryan K'd 383 batters.

183 **Yes.** The old Boston Braves somehow managed to get through nine doubleheaders in a row and set the record for playing consecutive twin bills. The year was 1928 and those unforgettable games were played between September 4-15.

184 **(C) The 1960 White Sox** was baseball's first major league to identify the players with their uniforms. Sox owner Bill Veeck had the idea in order for the fans to be able to cheer for Kluszewski, Minoso, Aparicio and Nellie Fox, to name a few.

185 **(D)** Talk about playing the spoiler. **Horace Clarke** of the Yanks in 1970 was the kiss of death for those hard luck pitchers. Clarke hit .251 but can say that at least three of them were timely.

186 **(D) Hall of Famer Sam Rice** *was* the Senators. His career spanned from 1915 to 1934 and all

ANSWERS 109

but one of those years with the Washington club. Rice saw action in 2,307 games, went to bat close to 9,000 times, managed 2,889 hits (478 doubles, 183 triples) and scored 1,467 times for Washington.

187 **(B) The Yankees** managed to leave 20 runners stranded in a game against Boston on September 21, 1956.

188 **(B)** Before the next pitch, the team in the field can appeal the play and ask the umpire for a decision. If the umpire saw the mistake and the team in the field had the ball at the base which the player failed to touch, he would be called out.

189 **Yes.** Milt Pappas, who saw time in both the American and National Leagues, finished his career with a total of 209 victories, but managed to win only 16 games in one season for his top mark.

190 **(B) Major Leaguer, Roy Smalley** is the son of Roy Smalley, Sr. and the nephew of Gene Mauch.

191 **(A)** Wilson's mark of 58 homers for the 1930 season topped Chuck Klein's 1926 total of 43 while with the Phillies.

192 **(C)** More than 100 but less than 150. **Exactly 123**; that includes his highest single year total of seventeen in 1923.

193 **(B)** The record for most homers in one game is **eight.** This home run feat has been accomplished by the '53 Milwaukee Braves, '61 San Francisco Giants, '56 Cincinnati Reds, '63 Minnesota Twins, the '39 N.Y. Yankees,

'78 Montreal Expos' and '77 Boston Red Sox.

194 (B) Eddie Collins stole the show and **six** bases back in 1912 on a September afternoon. The footnote to the record is that Collins tied his own record eleven days later by again stealing six bases.

195 (C) Roric Harrison of Baltimore became the last pitcher to hit a round-tripper before the designated hitter rule. The historic event took place in Cleveland on October 3, 1972.

196 Yes. He hit only one, but it was quite a story. On September 13, 1946 in Cleveland, the Splendid Splinter connected in the first inning with a drive to left field. It was the pennant clinching game and the score was 1-0 with Williams' homer being the deciding factor.

197 (D) The American League record for successful sacrifice bunts is held by William Bradley with 46. Bradley was playing for Cleveland in 1907 when he set the record. In the National League, the record is held by William Gleason with 43 while playing for Philadelphia in 1905.

198 (A) The record is held by many catchers with a total of **six** foul ball put-outs.

199 (C) In 1916, while pitching for Philadelphia, Hall of Famer **Grover Cleveland Alexander** threw 16 shut-outs at the opposition.

200 (C) Ron Hunt holds the honors of being hit the most times with 227 times to his credit. The American League record is held by Minnie Minoso with 189 times.

201 (B) In a regular nine-inning contest, the

Dodgers once sent up **nine** pinch hitters while playing the Cards on September 22, 1959. In an extra-inning contest, the record is held by Oakland which sent ten pinch hitters against the White Sox on September 17, 1972.

202 (D) Yankee superstar and Hall of Famer **Mickey Mantle** was waiting in the on-deck circle when the McDougal-Score accident occurred. What most fans don't recall is that the center fielder for the Indians that day was another soon-to-be Yankee great, Roger Maris.

203 (A) Washington pitcher, Tom Zacharey, who threw the pitch that Babe hit for his 60th homer, was lifted in the ninth inning for a pinch hitter who was none other than **Walter Johnson.** This was Johnson's last appearance in the majors. He failed to get a base hit.

204 (A) Cleon Jones had the club theft mark of 16.

205 1. Old Arbitrator   E. Bill Klem
      2. Old Fox   D. Clark Griffith
      3. Old Hoss   A. Charles Radbourn
      4. Old Roman   B. Charles Comiskey
      5. Old Stubblebeard   C. Burleigh Grimes

206 (B) Reggie Jackson.

207 (A) The **1916 New York Giants** had a winning streak of 26 games. Also included in that record was a tie game. It should be noted that the 26 games were all played at home. What a homestand!

208 (D) Hammerin Hank played long enough to play in different parks of the same team. In total, the answer is 23 parks in the National League. And for his short stay in the

American League, you can add another nine stadiums.

209 (B) Wes Ferrell finished his career with a lifetime batting average of .280. Ferrell not only hit for average, but had some power, ending up with a total of 38 home runs.

210 (D) In 1950, while playing for the Chicago White Sox, **Gus Zernial** tore up the American League hitting four homers in the month of October for the major league record. His 1950 home run total was 29.

211 (B) The record is **two,** when the A's victimized the Indians on July 25, 1930. The team was managed by Connie Mack as they finished in first place that year by eight games. Also on the team that holds the record for triple steals in one game were such noteworthy players as Jimmy Foxx, Max Bishop, Jimmy Dykes, Al Simmons, Mickey Cochrane, and Lefty Grove.

212 Bob Gibson of the St. Louis Cardinals.

213 (C) The record for hitting safely in most consecutive games was held by George Sisler of the old St. Louis Browns back in 1922 when the Hall of Famer hit safely in 41 games. This was the modern day record that DiMaggio broke. He also crashed the pre-1900 record held by Willie "Hit 'em Where They Ain't" Keeler.

214 (D) Dick Williams managed the 1967 Red Sox in the World Series but lost to the St. Louis Cardinals.

215 (C) Boston Hall of Famer Ted Williams, who was considered by many to be the last true student of the art of hitting, struck out a total

ANSWERS 113

of 709 times while having 7,706 career at-bats. Other statistics to consider would be the fact that the Splendid Splinter walked 2,018 times. In 1941, the year Williams hit .406, he fanned 27 times in 456 official at-bats.

216 **(B)** Only eight players have won the triple crown, with two of them accomplishing it twice. Comparing the statistics of each winner, a leader in each department can be found. The batting average title goes to **Rogers Hornsby** with .403 while the triple crown home run title goes to Mickey Mantle with 52, and Jimmy Foxx leads with 163 RBI. Hornsby, who won the triple crown twice would have to be the winner for the best of all triple crown winners with his 1922 statistics. The Rajah batted .401, hit 42 homers and drove in 152 runs.

217 **(B)** Pat Corrales owns it. The year was 1965 when Corrales was playing with the Philadelphia Phillies. Corrales played in 63 games and was awarded first base a record **six** times due to catcher's interference. Catcher's interference usually means that the catcher touched the hitter's bat with his glove during the swing.

218 **(B) Ron Blomberg** of the New York Yankees in 1973.

219 **(C) Ray Narleski** was on the other end of four grand slams in 1959 while pitching for the Detroit Tigers. Narleski had a final record of 4-12 that season and an ERA of 5.78. It isn't known to this day if those grand slams had anything to do with the fact that Narleski decided to hang 'em up after that 1959 season, his sixth in the majors.

220 (D) Tip O'Neill of the St. Louis club in the American Association did it all in 1887 with 14 homers, 19 triples, 52 doubles, 167 runs scored, .435 batting average, 357 total bases, and a slugging average of .691.

221 1. Nippy Jones   E. Vernal
2. Mickey Owen   D. Arnold
3. Cookie Cavagetto   A. Harry
4. Pumpsie Green   B. Elijah
5. Randy Hundley   C. Cecil
6. Birdie Tebbetts   F. George

222 (D) Since 1899, the record belongs to **Jimmy Dykes with a piloting total of six teams.** Dykes started his managerial career with the 1934 White Sox and stayed until 1946. Along the line, Dykes also managed the Philadelphia A's from 1951-53, Baltimore Orioles in 1954, the Cincinnati Reds in 1958, Detroit Tigers in 1959-60, and finally Cleveland Indians in the 1960-61 seasons.

223 True. Baker received his nickname from the 1911 World Series in which he hit one home run in games two and three.

224 (A) Norm and Larry Sherry. Rick Ferrell was a catcher when he hit his homer off brother Wes. George Stoval in 1940 was with Cleveland when he connected off of brother Jesse who was pitching for Detroit. The most recent brother combination was the Niekro brothers. Joe, while playing for Houston connected with one off of brother Phil, who was pitching for Atlanta on May 29, 1976.

225 (B) The American League record is also the major league record in that department. A total of 11 walks were recorded in a game played by the old St. Louis Browns against

ANSWERS 115

the New York Yankees. It was the Browns on August 1, 1941 who could not get a run even though they received 11 walks. The National League record is held by the Reds with nine when they played the Cards on September 1, 1958.

226 (A) A player playing all nine positions in one game has happened only **twice.** Bert Campaneris, while with the Kansas City A's did it in 1965 and in 1968 Cesar Tovar of the Minnesota Twins did it again. There have been players, however, who over the course of a season, played all nine positions. In fact, it has been done seven times, the first time occuring in the season of 1899 by Lewis McAllister of the Cleveland National League club.

227 (C) It's **James Galvin** who pitched before 1900 and worked over 70 complete games in both 1883 and 1884. Pud won a total of 361 games and lost only 309.

228 (C) Cobb batted .326 while facing Ruth in those 13 contests.

229 (C) William Gray of Washington walked seven straight batters in the first inning of a game on August 28, 1909.

230 (C) Gene Stephens, after pinch running for Ted Williams stayed in the lineup and had his turn at bat come up as the Red Sox went around the batting order on July 13, 1959. Stephens took advantage of the at-bat and hit a grand slam.

231 (C) Joltin' **Joe DiMaggio** hit into three double plays in the 11 games he played to hold the record for All-Star play.

116 THE BASEBALL QUIZ BOOK

232 (B) Warren Spahn played for Casey Stengel in 1942 while with the Boston Braves which finished in 7th place and then again in 1965 when both were on the Mets. The Mets finished in last place. Stengel also worked for the Yanks as their manager and turned in 10 pennant winners.

233 Al Downing.

234 (C) 5'5" Freddie Patek said it. The little shortstop broke into the majors in 1968 with the Pirates.

235 (D) At the tail end of the 1948 season, the Brooklyn Dodgers were searching for a new radio broadcaster and a deal was struck between the club and the Atlanta Crackers. The swap saw the Dodgers get Ernie Harwell (who was broadcasting the Crackers' games) and in return they sent the Crackers catcher Cliff Dapper. Harwell is still in the majors broadcasting games for the Detroit Tigers. Dapper, on the other hand, only got to see eight games in the majors and has faded from the memories of most. By the way, in case you're wondering, as of 1983, a World Series game has not been rained out once it started; no female has played major league baseball; and Connie Mack won 3,776 games and lost 4,025 as a manager.

236 (C) Dick Littlefield, Bob L. Miller, and Tommy Davis each had the pleasure of seeing action with ten major league teams for the record. Littlefield was the first player to accomplish this dubious distinction when he played for the Red Sox, White Sox, Tigers, Browns, Orioles, Pirates, Cards, Giants, Cubs, and

Braves. The interesting part of the record is that it took Littlefield only nine years to set this record while Miller had to play 17 years and Davis played 18 years.

237 **(B)** Harry Anderson of the Phillies, the date was September 3, 1957 and the losing pitcher was Don Drysdale in a 3-2 Dodger loss.

238 **(A)** As far as rookies are concerned, the top mark in homers is 38. This mark has been reached twice, first by Wally Berger in 1930 and then by Frank Robinson in 1956. Both National Leaguers were outfielders and did pretty well in the average department. Berger hit .310 in his rookie season while Robinson hit .290. Over in the American League, the rookie home run mark is held by Al Rosen with 37 while playing for Cleveland in the 1950 season.

239 **(C)** Babe Ruth hit two or more homers 72 times in his career.

240 **(D)** The record stands at four strikeouts for one inning and it is held by 14 different pitchers. In all of the situations, one of the strikeouts was a dropped third strike and the batter reached base safely but no out was recorded. Ed Crane of the New York Giants was the first National Leaguer to make the exclusive four strikeouts in one inning club. He did it on October 4, 1888 in the fifth inning. Other notable pitchers to tie the record are Joe Nuxhall of Cincy in 1959, Don Drysdale of the Dodgers in 1965, Bob Gibson of the Cards in 1966 and Mike Cuellar of the Orioles in 1970.

241 Truck Hannah (1918-20)　Eddie Kazak (1949-52)
　　Tobby Harrah (1960 -)　　Dick Nen (1963-70)

242 **Tony C. was 22** years old at the time.

243
1. Rick Dempsey — F. John
2. Buck Dent — E. Russell
3. Ken Griffey — A. George
4. Mike Hargrove — C. Dudley
5. Bob Horner — B. James
6. Bruce Sutter — D. Howard

244 **(B)** Chicago was playing Detroit of the National League back on September 6, 1883 and scored the unbelievable record of **18** runs in the seventh inning.

245 1B George Sisler (1922) .420
2B Rogers Hornsby (1924) .424
SS Luke Appling (1936) .388
3B Fred Lindstrom (1930) .379
OF Ty Cobb (1911) .420
C Bill Dickey (1936) .362
P Walter Johnson (1925) .440 (in 30 games)

246 In 1932, **Chuck Klein** won the MVP award in the National League for the Phillies and in 1933 Klein won the Triple Crown only to be traded to the Chicago Cubs.

247 **True.** Ralph Kiner and Johnny Mize hit the same number of round-trippers in 1947 (51 homers) and in 1948 (40 homers).

248 Tovar only pitched one game in his career. In 1968, while with the Twins, he started one game and pitched one inning. He walked one batter, did not give up any hits and struck out one — **Reggie Jackson** of Oakland.

249 **(C)** The catcher was Detroit's backstop, **Bill Freehan,** with 9,629 putouts.

ANSWERS 119

250 **(B) Seven:** Yogi Berra, Billy Hunter, Eddie Lopat, Billy Martin, Hank Bauer, Ralph Houk, Jerry Coleman.

251 **True.** Johnny Clements, who caught 1,073 games, saw the most action among left handed receivers. He played with the Phillies (1885-1887), St. Louis (1898), Cleveland (1899), and Boston (1900).

252 **(D)** There is a record for players playing a minimum 150 games with the fewest strikeouts. Joe Sewell of Cleveland came the closest when he struckout **four** times in 1925 and played in 155 games. The amazing thing about Sewell is the fact that in 1929, while playing in 152 games, he again struckout only four times. In fact, Sewell's lifetime mark for strikeouts is 114 while having 7,132 at-bats. It's no wonder that he is in baseball's Hall of Fame.

253 **(A)** It was back in **1926** on August 28. The pitcher involved was Emil Levsen of Cleveland when the Indians beat Boston with scores of 6-1 and 5-1.

254 **(C)** Minnesota's **Dan Ford** hit the first homer at the new stadium April 5, 1976.

255 **(C)** The record is **24** runs and the unfortunate pitcher's name was Aloysius Travers. He pitched for the Detroit Tigers in 1912 and wound up giving up 26 hits and 7 bases on balls. His ERA was a cool 15.75. It won't come as any surprise that this was Traver's first and only game in the majors.

256 **Billy Hamilton, Billy Evans, Billy Herman.**

257 (B) Mickey Mantle connected against the Dodgers on October 4, 1953 to become the second player in World Series competition to hit a grand slam.

258 (D) Garry Maddox.

259 1. The People's Cherce   E. Dixie Walker
2. The Springfield Rifle   F. Vic Raschi
3. The Old Arbitrator   D. Bill Klein
4. The Fordham Flash   C. Frank Frisch
5. The Kid   B. Ted Williams
6. The Hammer   A. Hank Aaron

260 (B) Ralph Kiner said it and backed it up with 369 homers and who knows how many Cadillacs.

261 (B) Joey Jay, who started out in the little leagues, appeared in the 1961 World Series when the Reds took on the Yanks. Jay appeared in the October 5 game for Cincinnati.

262 (B) Hank Aaron.

Section IV
Answer Worksheet

ANSWER WORKSHEET

1. _____
2. _____
3. _____
4. _____
5. _____
6. _____
7. _____
8. _____
9. _____
10. _____
11. _____
12. _____
13. _____
14. _____
15. _____
16. _____
17. _____
18. _____
19. _____
20. _____
21. _____
22. _____
23. _____
24. _____
25. _____
26. _____
27. _____
28. _____
29. _____
30. _____
31. _____
32. _____
33. _____
34. _____
35. _____
36. _____
37. _____
38. _____
39. _____
40. _____
41. _____
42. _____
43. _____
44. _____

124 THE BASEBALL QUIZ BOOK

45. _____
46. _____
47. _____
48. _____
49. _____
50. _____
51. _____
52. _____
53. _____
54. _____
55. _____
56. _____
57. _____
58. _____
59. _____
60. _____
61. _____
62. _____
63. _____
64. _____
65. _____
66. _____

67. _____
68. _____
69. _____
70. _____
71. _____
72. _____
73. _____
74. _____
75. _____
76. _____
77. _____
78. _____
79. _____
80. _____
81. _____
82. _____
83. _____
84. _____
85. _____
86. _____
87. _____
88. _____

ANSWER WORKSHEET

89. _____	111. _____
90. _____	112. _____
91. _____	113. _____
92. _____	114. _____
93. _____	115. _____
94. _____	116. _____
95. _____	117. _____
96. _____	118. _____
97. _____	119. _____
98. _____	120. _____
99. _____	121. _____
100. _____	122. _____
101. _____	123. _____
102. _____	124. _____
103. _____	125. _____
104. _____	126. _____
105. _____	127. _____
106. _____	128. _____
107. _____	129. _____
108. _____	130. _____
109. _____	131. _____
110. _____	132. _____

126 THE BASEBALL QUIZ BOOK

133. _____
134. _____
135. _____
136. _____
137. _____
138. _____
139. _____
140. _____
141. _____
142. _____
143. _____
144. _____
145. _____
146. _____
147. _____
148. _____
149. _____
150. _____
151. _____
152. _____
153. _____
154. _____

155. _____
156. _____
157. _____
158. _____
159. _____
160. _____
161. _____
162. _____
163. _____
164. _____
165. _____
166. _____
167. _____
168. _____
169. _____
170. _____
171. _____
172. _____
173. _____
174. _____
175. _____
176. _____

ANSWER WORKSHEET

177. _____   199. _____
178. _____   200. _____
179. _____   201. _____
180. _____   202. _____
181. _____   203. _____
182. _____   204. _____
183. _____   205. _____
184. _____   206. _____
185. _____   207. _____
186. _____   208. _____
187. _____   209. _____
188. _____   210. _____
189. _____   211. _____
190. _____   212. _____
191. _____   213. _____
192. _____   214. _____
193. _____   215. _____
194. _____   216. _____
195. _____   217. _____
196. _____   218. _____
197. _____   219. _____
198. _____   220. _____

128 THE BASEBALL QUIZ BOOK

221. _____   242. _____
222. _____   243. _____
223. _____   244. _____
224. _____   245. _____
225. _____   246. _____
226. _____   247. _____
227. _____   248. _____
228. _____   249. _____
229. _____   250. _____
230. _____   251. _____
231. _____   252. _____
232. _____   253. _____
233. _____   254. _____
234. _____   255. _____
235. _____   256. _____
236. _____   257. _____
237. _____   258. _____
238. _____   259. _____
239. _____   260. _____
240. _____   261. _____
241. _____   262. _____

About the Authors

Ted Giannoulas

In the time honored phrase, The Famous Chicken needs no introduction. He has been delighting and charming audiences in the millions these past years in a truly unprecedented way and most of them are baseball fans. As it turns out, Ted Giannoulas, The Famous Chickens' alter ego, is also a baseball fan. In conjunction with his friend Andy Strasberg, he has written a baseball quiz or trivia book.

Andy Strasberg

Strasberg, Director of Marketing, San Diego Padres, is above and beyond the call of duty, a student of baseball history, a collector of baseball memorabilia and a repository of baseball facts and figures.